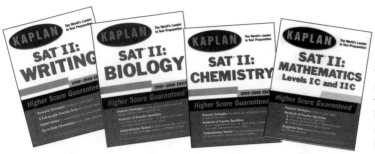

HIGH SCHOOL 411

by Cynthia Hickman

Simon & Schuster

Kaplan Books

Published by Kaplan Educational Centers and Simon & Schuster

1230 Avenue of the Americas

New York, NY 10020

Copyright © 1999 by Kaplan Educational Centers

For bulk sales to schools, colleges, and universities, please contact Renee Nemire, Simon & Schuster Markets, 1633 Broadway, 8th Floor, New York, NY 10019.

Kaplan® is a registered trademark of Kaplan Educational Centers.

ACT® is a registered trademark of the American College Testing Program.

College Board, Advanced Placement Program, College-Level Examination Program, College Scholarship Service (CSS), Profile, SAT I and SAT II are all registered trademarks of the College Entrance Examination Board.

Editor: Amy Arner Sgarro

Cover Design: Cheung Tai

Interior Page Design and Layout: Mike Shevlin and Vincent Jeffrey

Production Editor: Maude Spekes

Managing Editor: Dave Chipps

Executive Editor: Del Franz

Special thanks to Cheri Eddy, Judi Knott, Jessica Meo, Sara Pearl, Donna Ratajczak, Julia Rimann, Daniel Shack, and Sumi Wong.

Manufactured in the United States of America

Published Simultaneously in Canada

October 1999

10 9 8 7 6 5 4 3 2 1

Library of Congress Cataloging-in-Publication Data is available.

ISBN: 0-684-86611-0

About the Author

Cynthia Hickman attended public schools in New York City and earned an A.B., M.B.A., and J.D. from Harvard University. She is a former student recruiter for Harvard/Radcliffe Colleges. Cynthia has been admitted to practice law in the State of New York and, in recent years, has launched top-rated educational sites on the Internet and America Online™ while developing study skills, career, test-prep, admissions, and financial aid software on CD-ROM for an educational publisher.

Acknowledgments

I would like to thank my classmates and friends Darryl Goodwin, Darrick Grimes, Kathy Henderson, Dr. Jason Mack, Vanessa Richardson, Terri Walker, Lissa Williams, Capt. Elvis Vasquez; and my teachers and advisors Martin Block, Sydney Farber, Raymond Goldfeder, Judith Goldman, William Ma, Joanne Panzarella-Megna, and Alice Smith for making my high school years memorable. To Mrs. Bernice Clark: If only all headstrong, inquiring minds had such great, indulging starts. I would also like to thank Carla Harris, Kelli Holden, Alvaro Martin, and Dr. Rochelle Rothstein for their interest, comments, and support.

This book is dedicated to my mother and E. E.

Table of Contents

Introduction

All parents want to help their children make the most of their high school years, especially since a student's high school record greatly impacts college admissions. Yet many parents make the mistake of getting involved too late in the game. Getting into the college of choice begins on the first day of class in high school. Admissions officers look at students' courses, grades, test scores, and activities throughout high school years. They also look to see whether a student has demonstrated those personal qualities that will make him a welcome addition to their campus. That's where this book comes in. *High School 411* will show you what opportunities are available for your child, at school and in your community. From figuring out which courses to take, how to best prepare for tests, and which extracurriculars to pursue, this step-by-step guide helps you help your child make the most of—and enjoy—his high school years, with an eye towards getting into the college of his choice.

High School 411 provides a glimpse into what resources you and your teenager can draw upon to make her high school years as successful as they deserve to be. To that end, we've included hundreds of Internet listings, as well as mail, phone, and fax contacts, that can help students manage homework, get information on colleges, and pursue individual interests. We've also provided tips from high-achieving teens on what they, and their parents, did to make their high school years a success. Finally, we asked guidance counselors to pass on their advice about what parents can do to help their high schoolers excel.

How you choose to guide your child through these notoriously difficult years depends on each of your personal styles. You may find that your son needs some extra encouragement in trying new activities or choosing challenging classes. Or he might be quite independent, giving you less information than you might like about school and afterschool activities. Whatever your and your teenager's inclinations and needs, *High School 411* can help you answer questions frequently asked by students and their parents about high school. Together, you can set goals and make choices that lead to a successful high school career.

CHAPTER 1

Classes

WHAT STUDENTS ASK

- **What classes should I take?**
- **What programs are available for motivated students?**
- **Are there alternatives to my local high school?**

Your child is going to be spending the majority of his high school hours sitting in class. That's why the classes he chooses have such a huge impact on his experience of high school, as well as on his chances of getting into the college of his choice. Your son's choice of classes (and his performance in them) reveals whether he is academically prepared, intellectually curious, and up to the challenge of taking progressively harder courses or participating in innovative school programs—all important criteria to college admissions committees.

As he plans his high school classes, your teenager's focus should be on meeting high school graduation requirements as well as college admissions requirements. But he should also concentrate on taking courses that stimulate him and that he'll enjoy. And the best way to do this is to create a study plan for his high school years. For your child, creating a study plan means taking some control of the high school experience, setting goals, and finding a practical way of meeting them.

As a parent, you can, and should, help your child choose classes that will stimulate him, and help him increase his chances of getting in to the colleges of his choice. You can help him look at the big picture, and with him, plan the course of his high school years. Your child's guidance counselor can help make you aware of the courses offered, those best suited to your child, and the requirements for graduation as well as for college admission.

CREATING A STUDY PLAN

A study plan is a schedule of all the classes your son wants and needs to take while in high school. These classes include basic subjects like science, math, English, and social studies, as well as other subjects like foreign language, music, and art. Developing a study plan helps him to identify the course requirements for graduation and college admissions, as well as what classes are available at his school to meet them. But it also helps him—and you—understand his interests a little better, and can lend a hand in figuring out what direction he wants to take in college and beyond.

Consider the following five factors when developing a study plan:

- graduation requirements
- college admissions requirements
- class availability
- academic interests
- creating a sequence

By thoroughly investigating these issues, your child will be able to start on the best possible academic plan for his high school years.

Graduation Requirements

It may seem obvious, but you can't go to college until you get out of high school. During your daughter's freshman year, she should schedule a meeting with her guidance counselor to find out about her school's academic requirements for graduation by subject area, years of study, and classes to be completed.

Most high schools have the following requirements for graduation:

HIGH SCHOOL GRADUATION REQUIREMENTS

Subject	Minimum Years of Study	Classes
English	3	Composition (minimum 1 year) and literature (minimum 1 year)
Mathematics	2	Algebra and geometry
Sciences	2	Including biology
Social Studies	2	American history
Foreign Language	2	Same language

How does your daughter's school's graduation requirements match up to this example? Tracking Sheet 1.1 at the end of this chapter can help you compare.

College Admissions Requirements

High school graduation requirements aren't all that students have to contend with: Top colleges and universities have admissions requirements for classes to be completed in high school. These requirements vary by college, but all are there to represent those classes the college or university believes best prepares a student for success at their school. If your child plans to attend a top college, her admission requirements will probably look like this:

RECOMMENDED PROGRAM OF STUDY FOR TOP COLLEGES

Subject	Minimum Years of Study	Classes
English	4	Minimum of 2 years in composition with 1+ year(s) of literature
Foreign Language	3	One foreign language
Mathematics	3	Through trigonometry (including advanced algebra and/or calculus)
Sciences	3	Three years of lab sciences (e.g., biology, chemistry, and physics)
Social Studies	3	American and world studies
Arts and Music	1	

Clearly, if your child is thinking about applying to a competitive college or university, satisfying graduation requirements might not be enough to meet the admissions criteria. She can find out what courses her target colleges require by writing away for an admissions booklet, or by consulting one of the comprehensive guides to colleges in her school library or local bookstore.

There are other reasons your child should take tougher courses. More advanced classes help develop key skills like writing, critical reading, and problem solving—basic skills needed in college, as well as later on at work. Also, most of the highest scorers on the college entrance exams like the SAT I are students who have completed or exceeded admissions requirements. Give her every possible advantage for college admissions and build a study plan that includes the most challenging admissions requirements that you find when researching her target schools.

TEN SCHOOLS WITH TOUGH ADMISSIONS REQUIREMENTS*

Bennington

Brown

Emory

Georgia Institute of Technology

Kent State

NYU

Syracuse

University of Florida

University of Georgia

University of North Carolina at Chapel Hill

* Require at least three years of science and math and two of a foreign language. Many other schools also have stringent admissions requirements.

Practical Stuff

There are other, more practical courses a student should take aside from those required for graduation and admission. All college-bound students should learn to use a personal computer; this includes gaining a working knowledge of both word processing and database software programs. Using a personal computer will help when writing and editing papers and conducting research from online databases or encyclopedias on CD-ROM. And students should consider taking a typing course. The arrangement of the keyboard for both machines is similar—your computer will work only as fast as you can click and type. Finally, students should take a class on how to conduct research if such a class is available; it could help them learn how to develop an outline for research and writing, how to use the library and other sources to gather data, how to structure arguments and write logically, and how to use footnotes and bibliographies.

STARTING THE PLAN

He's gotten graduation requirements from his guidance counselor and knows his target colleges' admissions requirements. Armed with these, it's time to start forming a study plan. Your first step: Together, look at both sets of requirements and note the set of requirements that is greater in areas of study (e.g., adding physical education), requires a higher number of years of study (e.g., three years of math instead of two), and has the greater class requirements (e.g., two years of composition instead of one).

CONSOLIDATED REQUIREMENTS
An Example

Subject	Minimum Years of Study	Classes
English	4	2 years of composition, 1 year of literature, 1 year of electives
Social Studies	3	3 years of electives
Mathematics	3	3 or 4 years, through calculus
Sciences	3	3 years of laboratory sciences (e.g., biology, chemistry, and physics)
Foreign Language	3	3 years of same language
Art and Music	1	
Physical Education	4	
Other	1	Typing and Computers

Since juggling two sets of requirements can be confusing, use the tracking sheet at the end of this chapter to help you figure out how to meet your child's needs.

Class Availability

Next, you'll need to find out what classes your son's school offers. His school's guidance office should be able to help you here. What does he need to take? Will he be able to take the classes he needs when he'd like to take them? Competition for seats in popular courses can be fierce; in some schools, spaces for advanced courses often go to upperclassmen first, leaving motivated underclassmen to wait several semesters or years before they can get in. Then there's a scheduling problem: AP Physics and French 3 may both be offered at the same time, forcing him to choose between the two. This means that he'll have to develop a flexible study plan with several ways to meet his critical requirements while taking courses that interest him. Remind him that it's better to be safe than to assume that he'll get into a specific class or section when he wants or needs to.

Academic Interests

Seventy-five to 90 percent of your daughter's classes in high school will be used to meet the requirements for graduation and college admissions. The remaining 10–25 percent of classes are electives. How to choose classes in required subjects? How do you decide which electives to take? For example, do you take economics, government, U.S. history, or something else to satisfy your social studies requirement? Do you take French, Spanish, or Latin to satisfy a language requirement? A common sense rule of thumb: Let your child's interests be her guide.

Below are two exercises to help your daughter find those subject areas and classes that interest her the most. Remember that she'll do best in classes that interest her—if she enjoys her classes, chances are she'll study longer and get better grades. So don't suggest that she take advanced accounting if the mere thought of it makes her queasy: She'll probably bomb the class, and hate the whole experience.

Here's how to start. If your child is so inclined do the exercises together. For the first exercise, answer the following questions.

Exercise 1—Define Your Interests
- What do you like to do in your free time?
- What books do you like to read?
- What parts of the world (or universe) interest you the most?
- If you had to choose a career today, what would it be? Why?

For example, a student who likes to read science fiction, keep an aquarium, and watch *The X-Files*, and is considering a career in marine biology is pretty clearly science oriented, and should focus on sciences in her study plan. Though your child's interests may be more diverse and less easy to read, they should give you a strong sense as to where her interests congregate and what she'd be happiest studying.

Exercise 2—Academic Areas of Interest
In this exercise you and your child identify his academic interests by subject area. On a scale of 0 to 5, rank each subject area. A zero represents no interest, while a five indicates great interest. Find out the average rating of each area by adding the scores by category, then dividing the total by the number of subjects rated in each category.

This exercise tells you two things about your child's interests: first, the subject areas in which she has the strongest interest, indicated by an average score of four or five. For these areas, she should take more, or advanced, classes. Second, the subject areas ranked zero, one, or two are areas in which she has the lowest level of interest. She should avoid these areas, if possible, once she's completed the minimum requirements for graduation and admissions. Try to find classes that are somehow related to those areas that she likes a lot; for example, she might be able to take geography instead of postindustrial Europe for her social studies requirement if she is science minded.

After you've done both exercises, look for similarities in the results; you should see some consistency.

Creating a Sequence

A sequence of classes usually begins with an introductory class followed by advanced courses that cover more complex principles. In your child's study plan, choose classes that begin at a level at which she can follow and appreciate the materials being taught. She shouldn't choose courses that are too easy; she might be bored out of her mind, and won't do nearly as well as expected. On the other hand, she shouldn't jump right into impressive-sounding advanced courses she's not prepared for. As she completes each course, she should ask herself if she's up to taking a more advanced course that builds on what she's just learned. If she can and it's an area in which she has some interest, tell her to go for it—demonstrate her ability to do more difficult work. If she can't (and the course isn't needed to satisfy a requirement), she should move on to another class or subject area that will provide her with both a new and a greater challenge.

Your child should try to complete most of his class requirements by the end of his junior year. This timing helps to meet several goals: First, he can show academic achievement and preparedness when he applies to college in the fall of his senior year. Second, he can give himself a good shot at doing well on the standardized exams (e.g., SAT I and ACT) because the math and verbal skills tested can be developed in these classes. These tests need to be taken tests by the first semester of senior year.

PROGRAM ALTERNATIVES

Does your child go to a great high school that offers a wide range of challenging courses? Consider yourself lucky. But what if his school isn't quite up to snuff? What if you can't find the range of courses (breadth), the number of advanced classes (depth), or the variety of special interest programs (reach) you want or need in your child's school's schedule of classes? He may have to work a little harder to get the classes he's after by looking into alternative academic programs inside and outside of his high school. If the gaps in his study plan are small, participating in an Advanced Placement (AP) program may be enough. If, however, the gaps are substantial, you may want to consider cross-registering him at a nearby "magnet" school, or attending other special programs to add to or replace his school's offerings.

Few students have to "make do" with the classes that are available at their local high schools. There are alternative programs all over the country. However, these opportunities often depend on your seeking them out. Your child might be able to supplement his plan through another nearby high school or community college. He might want to consider switching schools, going to boarding school, or taking summer classes.

WHAT DOES THE SCHOOL OFFER?

High schools in the United States offer a dizzying array of diploma options, including comprehensive, general, vocational, regents, honors, Advanced Placement, and International Baccalaureate (IB). Which diploma programs are offered at your son's or daughter's high school? This is something you should investigate early in his or her high school career. It can give you a clue as to the school's breath, depth, and reach of its schedule of classes.

Below are some of the more common diploma options available. See how your child's school matches up:

- **General/Comprehensive**

  Most high schools offer this course of study. It's standard fare, with few exceptions made for students with special needs and interests; these schools may also offer a limited number of advanced programs. Students are likely to be

> "Find out how academics work at the start of high school. Find out if there's a top ten, whether grades are weighted, what honors are available . . . but do it at the start."
>
> —High school senior, ranked in top 10 of graduating class

given a few "comprehensive" statewide exams with the remaining exams presented as finals and taken in class at the end of each school term.

- **Vocational/Arts**

  These are programs offered by select high schools. They're likely to offer a general/comprehensive program of study with additional courses available for specific vocations and/or the arts. Entrance into these programs is often based on a special application, audition, or presentation of a portfolio of work. Likewise, graduation is often based on completing the general program of study and a project, portfolio, or other performance piece.

- **Regents, Honors, AP, and/or IB**

  Schools offering these diplomas are likely to have a range of advanced courses in a number of subject areas. Students often take special statewide exams at the end of each advanced course and may also take nationally and internationally administered exams. Although participation in many honors programs is voluntary, it often requires proof of academic accomplishment in preliminary courses. Admission into some of these programs (or the schools offering them) is sometimes competitive and based on test scores and other admissions criteria. Upon successfully completing an honors program, students receive an honors diploma (e.g., Regents Diploma or IB Diploma) instead of the general degree received by all other students.

Your daughter may find that the programs her school offers meet her needs, perhaps with a bit of fine tuning. But she may be motivated to achieve more than what a general program can offer. If this is the case, below are some alternatives to consider as she builds her academic plan.

INTERNATIONAL BACCALAUREATE

One of the most comprehensive and challenging programs available to college-bound high school students is the International Baccalaureate (IB) diploma program, an honors program adopted by more than 500 high schools in over 71 countries around the world. The IB program consists of required courses, exams, and related activities during a student's last two years of high school. It represents one of the higher hurdles that thousands of students in the United States clear each year in order to complete an advanced study plan. Students completing the IB program and its qualifying exams receive an IB diploma that is recognized by schools as proof of academic readiness for college-level work. Receiving an IB diploma also often qualifies these students for college credit and advanced standing at elite colleges and universities.

The IB's curriculum is not based on any specific high school's graduation requirements or the graduation requirements of any one country. Instead, it is an advanced program for "students of the world" who want to participate in a program that gives them a global perspective on people, cultures, history, and events while meeting the academic requirements for admission to top colleges in almost every country around the world. It's an ambitious and rewarding program of study for students who want to get an early start on learning how to compete more effectively in our global work and living place.

IB Program Requirements

The subjects that make up the IB program fall into six groups. For American students, these groups are English (language and literature), a foreign language, social studies, science, math, and electives that range from art to computers to religion. All IB diploma candidates must study at least three areas at an advanced level, and may pursue up to four of them at this advanced level depending on their completion of preliminary courses.

The IB program has additional requirements. All students must complete a course called the Theory of Knowledge, a course that represents the philosophical backbone of the IB program and that focuses on integrating learning inside and outside of the classroom into a personal philosophy and approach to thinking critically and reaching sound conclusions; in other words, it teaches you how to think for yourself. Unlike the other courses in the IB program, the grade in this class is not determined by a internationally administered exam, but is determined and given by the class' teacher. For all other courses, students take annual exams in May and/or November of each year.

Another requirement for IB diploma candidates is the completion of an Extended Essay, or research paper, on a subject covered in the IB curriculum. This is similar to the senior research paper requirement found in some competitive colleges and universities. This paper must be the original work of the student, and should demonstrate (in under 4,000 words) an ability to think logically and present a well-reasoned argument.

THE IB PROGRAM REQUIREMENTS: A SUMMARY

Requirements	Notes
Study in Six Areas	At least three must represent advanced study.
• English	
• Foreign language	All students are required to study a foreign language.
• Social studies	
• Science	
• Math	
• Electives	
Theory of Knowledge	Course requirement
Extended Essay	Research paper on any topic found in the IB curriculum
Creativity, Action, Service (CAS)	Series of community-based activities

While the focus on the IB program is primarily academic, it also requires students to participate in community-service projects. The program encourages its students to provide a useful service to their communities, interact with people of diverse backgrounds and cultures, and engage in activities in which they can learn more about IB academic areas and pursue other interests outside of the classroom.

Getting into an IB Program

To participate in the IB program, you must attend an IB- member high school. More than 250 high schools in the United States currently offer the IB diploma program. Is your son's school a member? Ask his guidance counselor about availability and program requirements.

If his high school doesn't offer the IB diploma, look into finding a school that does. To start, contact the other high schools in your area and ask whether they offer the IB diploma—one of them just might. You can also contact the North American office of the IB program and ask for a list of participating high schools. The IB's North American office can send you general information on the IB program and a booklet on the IB college credit and advanced standing policies of colleges and universities in the United States. You can contact them at International Baccalaureate North America, 200 Madison Avenue, Suite 2007, New York, New York, 10016-3903; telephone (212) 696-4464; fax (212) 889-9242.

If your child is interested in participating in an IB program, he'll need to make a decision no later than his freshman year of high school. Since IB students take college-level courses, he'll have to take the necessary preliminary courses early in his high school career to be eligible for admission into the program. Also, if he decides to pursue an IB program but it is not offered through his current high school, he'll have to transfer to a school that does.

ADVANCED PLACEMENT CLASSES

Unlike the IB program, which offers an integrated course of study, the Advanced Placement program, or AP, is a series of stand-alone, content-based exams sponsored by The College Board. Through the AP program, your child can pursue college-level work and earn college credit while still in high school. Students can take one AP class or many, depending on their interests.

Each AP program is based on a single national syllabus that is equal to a first-year college course. According to data released by the College Board, about fifteen per cent of all college-bound students (not just seniors) enroll in an AP course. More than 400,000 students take an AP exam each year, each student taking an estimated 1.5 exams. That's not even a quarter of the more than 2 million students applying to college each year, which means that if you take an AP course, you're in a select group.

Since the AP course is taught at the college level, your daughter may want to take courses in those subject areas in which she plans advanced college study. This way she can begin to address college requirements while in high school. Enrollment in an AP course is voluntary in most schools. However, most schools won't allow you to enroll in an AP course unless you've taken all the prerequisites in that particular subject area. For this reason alone it is key that she identifies which AP courses she would like to take early in high school and build these foundation courses into her study plan.

AP SUBJECT AREAS

AP courses are available in the following subject areas:

- Art
  History of Art
  Studio Art (semester-long)
  Drawing Portfolio
  General Portfolio
- Biology
- Chemistry
- Computer Science
  A: Semester-long introduction
  AB: Year-long introduction
- Economics
  Microeconomics
  Macroeconomics
- English
  Language and Composition
  Literature and Composition
- French
  Language
  Literature
- German Language
- Government and Politics (semester-long)
  Comparative
  United States

- History
  European
  United States
- Latin
  Virgil
  Latin Literature
- Mathematics
  AB: Introductory calculus
  BC: Calculus including advanced topics
- Music Theory
- Physics
  B: Noncalculus
  C: Mechanics with calculus
  C: Electricity and Magnetism with calculus
- Psychology (semester-long)
- Spanish
  Language
  Literature

Taking AP Exams

The AP exams are given in May each year. In any year, a student may take as many AP exams as he or she likes, with the following exceptions: Computer Science A with Computer Science B, Calculus AB with Calculus BC, or Drawing with General Portfolio Art.

AP exams are scored on a scale of 1 to 5, 5 being (in the College Board's terms) "extremely well qualified," and 1 being "no recommendation." A 3 or better on the AP exam is usually needed to skip entry-level college courses. Some colleges, including Ivy League universities, will grant sophomore status to students passing enough AP exams with sufficiently high scores; obviously, this is a very effective way to cut college costs. Policies on accepting AP credit and granting sophomore standing based on AP scores vary from school to school, so contact your selected colleges to determine their policy for granting AP credit.

For more information on the Advanced Placement Program, including course descriptions, sample questions, colleges accepting AP scores, fees and exam schedules, contact: the Advanced Placement Program, P.O. Box 6670, Princeton, New Jersey 08541-6670; phone (609) 771-7300.

AP Versus IB Programs

Although both AP and IB programs offer advanced levels of study, there are differences between the two. The AP program is more focused on U.S. educational standards and is larger and more flexible than the IB program. The AP curriculum is developed nationally and based on the content covered by most U.S. colleges and universities in their first-year courses. The IB curriculum, on the other hand, does not focus on the educational requirements of any one nation.

Another difference is the relative flexibility in taking an AP course. Students can take an AP course at their high school or at any other school (e.g., high school, college, or summer program) that offers it. To participate in the IB program, a student must attend an IB-member school. While thousands of high schools, colleges, and other programs offer AP courses, only a couple of hundred high schools offer the IB program in the United States.

Finally, the IB program offers an intensive and integrated curriculum in which students must complete courses, exams, and related activity over a two-year period to be eligible to receive an IB diploma. In contrast, the AP program consists of a series of classes that students can pick and choose from. A student may take one or several AP courses during his or her high school career.

If your son is in an IB program, should he still take AP exams? If he is fortunate to attend a school that uses the AP curriculum for its IB program, he should definitely take advantage of it and take AP exams. More U.S. colleges and universities accept AP exam scores than IB program credits. Combining IB program participation with AP credit gives students the best of both worlds. They can pursue a challenging, integrated, and global plan of study in high school while meeting many U.S. college and university requirements for advanced standing and placement.

MAGNET SCHOOLS AND PROGRAMS

An alternative your child might consider is attending a special "magnet" school or program full or part time. Magnet high schools have a specific academic, special interest, or career focus to them. These special schools often take one of two forms. The first is a single high school that houses several smaller "academies." Each academy is built around a theme like science or the arts. They typically occupy a part of the building and have their own classrooms (and instructors) where classes that revolve around the theme are taught. The academy's teachers also supervise field trips and other projects that are theme related. For the many key academic areas like math, English, and science, the academy's students share classrooms and teachers with the rest of the building's student population. The academy programs allow students to have a "normal" high school experience with access to a wide range of classes in the traditional subject areas and a diverse student body while also allowing them to pursue key interests, in-depth, through exposure to special courses and activities.

The other form that the magnet school takes is a single-themed school for all of the students attending it. In New York City, for example, students can choose among high schools with the following themes: Automotive, Aviation, Art and Design, Business, Environment, Fashion and Design, Humanities, Law and Social Justice, Mathematics and Science, Performing Arts, and others. They range from schools with specific career interests (e.g., automotive and business), to special interests (e.g., the environment and performing arts), to academic interests (e.g., humanities and mathematics and science). Some schools require test scores or an audition for entrance, while other require only that student decides to attend it.

Keep in mind that there's a difference between a magnet school and a magnet program. In a magnet school, almost all of the students attend that school full time, while a magnet program often accepts students who attend other schools for their academic classes. The author of this book attended a magnet program while she was in high school. During the mornings, she attended one high school where she took her academic classes (e.g., math, science, English, and social studies). During the afternoon, she attended a magnet program in the performing arts at another high school where she took her special-interest classes (e.g., drama, dance, voice, and music theory). Each semester she received grades from the magnet program that were included on her report card with the grades from her academic classes. The credit for the courses taken at the magnet program also counted towards her graduation requirements. She found this to be the ideal way to have the best of both worlds: advanced, college-prep courses in the key academic areas and special instruction in the arts.

Whether your child has a special interest or not, it's a good idea to look into the magnet schools and programs offered in your area. Visit your school's guidance office and ask about these options. Some school districts keep a clearinghouse of information on school programs; see if one is available in your area. Also keep a lookout for school fairs that showcase the different alternatives. Like the author, your child too can find a way to meet admissions requirements while pursuing her special interests for graduation credit.

EXTENSION PROGRAMS

Colleges and universities across the United States now offer college-level courses through continuing education and extension programs. Some of these programs allow high school students to enroll in courses for high school and, in most instances, college-level credit. If your son needs one or a few college-level courses to prepare for the college-level exams, or if he would like to pursue advanced studies in subject areas of interest to him, this is another option open to him. These courses are generally offered during the evening and are held year-round. To find out about available courses and admissions requirements and fees, contact your local college or university.

> "If your school isn't up to par, look to your community college for classes."
>
> —High school senior, ranked in top 2 percent of graduating class

SUMMER PROGRAMS

Many colleges hold summer sessions specifically for high school students. These sessions range from rigorous academic programs for gifted students to those that are more like summer camp; they range in length from a couple of days to several weeks. Summer programs are a great way to expose yourself to life on a college campus. From choosing classes and living in dorm rooms to learning to complete assignments independently and on time, these programs provide students with a slice of college life while earning college credits. Although most courses offered in these programs are identical to the ones given to college students during the academic year, many programs are also specifically designed for high school students looking to polish their basic skills or prepare for upcoming admissions tests.

Northwestern University, for example, sponsors one of the oldest and largest summer programs for high school students through its National High School Institute (NHSI). Each summer at NU, more than 900 students participate in the NHSI's ten divisions. These schools include Creative Media Writing, Dance, Debate, Engineering Science, Journalism, Leadership, Lincoln-Douglas Debate, Music, Radio/TV/Film Production, and Theater Arts (Performance and Design/Technical).

Students attending NHSI live on campus and participate in programs that introduce them to college-level study while gaining practical, hands-on experience in their areas of interest. Fees for the NHSI include tuition, room, board, health services, field trips, group events, and other activities. The total cost runs up to several thousands of dollars and it does not include transportation to and from the campus in Evanston, Illinois. However, as is true with most summer programs, scholarships and other forms of financial assistance are available and are awarded on the basis of financial need and academic merit. Apply for financial aid if you need it to attend this or any other summer program. In recent years close to 40 percent of all students attending NHSI received some form of financial assistance. For more information about the National High School Institute at Northwestern University, its admissions requirements, academic programs, scholarships, and more, contact: Northwestern University Office of Summer Session, 2115 North Campus Drive, Evanston, IL 60208-2650; telephone (800) 346-3768; e-mail summer@nwu.edu.

If the summer program alternative is of interest to your son, he needs to decide what kind of experience he is interested in. Does he want to experience campus life? Look for a program at one of your target schools. This is a great way to get a birds-eye view of life on campus and a test drive of the food, courses, facilities, and the surrounding area. Does he want to prepare for college entrance exams? Choose a school offering test-prep programs. Is he interested in earning college credit? Be sure that his target schools are accepting credits earned at his summer program. Although hundreds of colleges and universities accept test scores (e.g., ACT, SAT, and AP) for placement in courses and eligibility for special programs (e.g., sophomore standing), many do not accept "credits" as a substitute for taking classes at their schools. Finally, does he just want to hang out and make friends? That's OK too, but beware: Some of these programs are pretty intense (classes and assignments six days a week). Make sure your child does his homework; his goals for summer and the objectives of his target summer program should be in synch.

First Steps

To participate in a college or university summer program, contact your child's target school to see if they sponsor programs for high school students. Ask for information on the application process (including the form, application fees, and academic requirements), the program (size, length, age requirements, living accommodations, and courses offered), and the availability of financial aid. There are hundreds of summer programs that high school students can participate in. On the next page is a list of 100 top colleges, universities and institutes in the United States offering summer programs for high school students.

STUDY FOR GIFTED STUDENTS

Your daughter can also pursue additional study through one of the many programs for gifted students. Often these programs allow students to take advanced courses in a wide range of subjects through computer-based instruction during the school year and in a classroom setting during the summer months. An example of one of these programs for gifted students is the CTY/EPGY Distance Learning Project (DLP). The DLP is a program sponsored jointly by two organizations for gifted students: The John Hopkins University Center for Talented Youth (CTY) and the Stanford University Education Program for Gifted Youth (EPGY). This partnership provides advanced courses to students in their homes and combines computer-based instruction through the use of CD-ROMs with individual tutoring through e-mail and over the phone.

The DLP courses are offered four times a year; students who take a DLP course receive a software package and printed materials through the mail. The DLP then links each student to a tutor at Stanford University. Each course covers standard high school math, science, and writing subjects. Advanced Placement courses are also offered (including Calculus, Physics—Mechanics, Physics—Electricity and Magnetism, and Expository Writing). To be eligible, you must be in the seventh grade or higher, apply and be accepted, pay the quarterly tuition (around $400), and have the necessary equipment and Internet access. Students who successfully complete a DLP course receive credit from Stanford's School of Continuing Studies and may also qualify for AP credit. For more information on the CTY/EPGY DLP, including a free catalog and application material, contact: CTY/DLP, CTY—Johns Hopkins, 3400 North Charles Street, Baltimore, MD, 21218; fax at (410) 516-0804; or e-mail at dlpcty@jhu.edu. You can also write to

100 COLLEGES, UNIVERSITIES, AND INSTITUTES WITH SUMMER PROGRAMS FOR HIGH SCHOOL STUDENTS

Alphabetized by State

AL: U. of Alabama—
Tuscaloosa
AZ: U. of Arizona—Tucson
Arizona State
CA: California State
Institute of Tech.
Occidental
Pepperdine
Scripps
U. of California—
Davis
U. of California—Los
Angeles
U. of California—
Riverside
U. of California—
Santa Barbara
CO: U.S. Air Force
Academy
CT: U. of Connecticut—
Storrs
Wesleyan
Yale
DE: U. of Delaware—
Newark
DC: American
Catholic
George Washington
Georgetown
FL: U. of Florida—
Gainesville
GA: Emory
IA: Ball State
DePauw
Indiana State
Indiana
U. of Notre Dame
IL: Northern Illinois
Northwestern
School of the Art
Institute of Chicago
U. of Illinois—Urbana-
Champaign
IA: Grinnell
U. of Iowa—Iowa City

KS: Kansas State
U. of Kansas
LA: Louisiana State
MA: Boston College
Boston University
Brandeis
Hampshire
Harvard
MIT
Mount Holyoke
Radcliffe
Tufts
U. of Massachusetts
Wellesley
MD: Johns Hopkins
U.S. Naval Academy
U. of Maryland—
College Park
MI: Michigan State
MO: Northeast Missouri
State
Southwest Missouri
State
U. of Missouri
MS: Macalester
Carleton
NC: Davidson
Duke
U. of North
Carolina—
Chapel Hill
NH: U. of New Hampshire
NJ: Rutgers
NY: Barnard
Cornell
Fashion Institute of
Technology
NYU
Parsons School of
Design
Pratt Institute
Rensselaer Polytechnic
Institute
Skidmore
Syracuse
Union
U.S. Military Academy

OH: Bowling Green State
Oberlin
Ohio State
U. of Cincinnati
OR: Portland State
U. of Oregon—
Eugene
PA: Carnegie Mellon
Dickinson
Franklin and Marshall
Pennsylvania State
U. of Pennsylvania
Ursinus
RI: Brown
Rhode Island School
of Design
SC: Clemson
TX: Southern Methodist
Texas A&M
Texas Tech
UT: U. of Utah
VT: Bennington
VA: College of William
and Mary
Marymount
U. of Virginia
Washington and Lee
WA: Pacific Lutheran U.
of Richmond
Washington State
Western Washington
WI: Lawrence

19

EPGY: The Education Program for Gifted Youth at EPGY, Ventura Hall, Stanford, CT 94305-4115; telephone (415) 329-9920; or fax (415) 329-9924.

Several top universities participate in a national Talent Identification Program (TIP) for gifted students. TIP consists of four regional talent-search programs for students in middle and high school who are recruited for TIP mostly on the basis of ACT and SAT I scores. The four regional programs are located at Duke University in North Carolina, Johns Hopkins in Maryland, Northwestern University in Illinois, and the University of Denver in Colorado.

Each TIP sponsor provides school-year and summer programs for its students. The summer programs include intensive classes. At Duke, for example, the summer students in the TIP program take one class per three week session in which they complete the equivalent of a year of high school or a semester of college-level work. Each class meets six days a week, Monday through Saturday. TIP sponsors also provide other programs like weekend classes during the school year and opportunities for study and travel abroad. For more information on TIP and its university sponsors, contact the following organizations:

Duke University Talent Identification Program
Box 90747
Durham, NC 27708-0747
(919) 684-3847

Center for Talented Youth
Johns Hopkins University
3400 North Charles Street
Baltimore, MD 21218
(410) 516-0337

Center for Talent Development
Northwestern University
2003 Sheridan Road
Evanston, IL 60208
(847) 491-3782

Rocky Mountain Talent Search
University of Denver
Wesley Hall, Room 200
Denver, CO 80208
(303) 871-2983

Other programs for academically gifted and talented students (offering programs in conjunction with Duke University):

Center for Gifted Studies
University of Southern Mississippi
Southern Station Box 8207
Hattiesburg, MS 39406-8207
(601) 266-5236

Center for Gifted Studies
Western Kentucky University
Bowling Green, KY 42101
(502) 745-6323

Programs for the Gifted and Talented
Northwestern State University
124 Russell Hall
Natchitoches, LA 71457
(318) 357-4500

Gifted Students Institute
Southern Methodist University
Box 382
Dallas, TX 75275-0382
(214) 768-5437 or SMU-KIDS

For additional information on programs for gifted students you can also contact the American Association for Gifted Children at 112 West Main Street, Suite 100, Durham, NC, 27701; phone (919) 683-1400. As these programs illustrate, your child can study at home, part time, taking classes that are not available at her high school. For more long-distance learning and gifted-student program options, see the Internet site listings at the end of this chapter.

SWITCHING SCHOOLS

After investigating the programs the local high school offers and exploring her own particular interests, your daughter might decide that her high school simply doesn't offer the program she needs, and that the gaps are too wide to fill by taking summer courses or extension courses. Switching schools is a big decision, but one that many students face each year. It's a decision that can have financial implications for the entire family. Ultimately, going to a school that meets her needs will make your child's high school experience much more positive, and will boost her chances of getting into the college of choice.

We've already discussed finding a local magnet school or school that offers an IB program. Another option is switching to a prep school.

The decision to attend a prep school is often a clear one. The local high school may be academically lacking, or your daughter may want to participate in a sports or arts program that isn't offered. Prep schools provide a wide range of classes and activities for students who are almost uniformly college bound. Admission to prep schools is often competitive, and students generally take an entrance exam.

Prep schools fall into three categories: nonsectarian (or not affiliated with a religious group), religious, and, in a few rare cases, public. The chief distinction between nonsectarian and religious prep schools is that students at religious schools are often required to meet class—and in some instances extracurricular—requirements in religion. Prep schools are often further divided into day and boarding schools. Students attending day schools live at home and commute to school, while boarding school students generally live on campus throughout the school year. The decision to attend a boarding school versus a day school is often driven as much by student preference as it is by cost.

The annual costs of attending a prep school can run from nothing at most public schools to more than $20,000 a year for tuition, room, board, and supplies at exclusive, private prep schools. Why should you consider private prep schools as a viable option when most parents would not pay this much money for a college education? Like many competitive colleges, private preparatory schools are often looking for interesting and motivated students of different backgrounds (including economically challenged) to round out their student population. As a result, these schools offer scholarships and other forms of financial aid to help admitted students meet their expenses. However, most high school students (and their parents) don't aggressively pursue these financial aid opportunities; as a result, many private schools do not exhaust their fund of scholarships each year. There is also a national movement underway to encourage financially strapped families to look into preparatory programs for their students. Many states now offer school choice programs supported by state-funded and independent scholarships. Although many of these programs don't pay full tuition costs, they offer grants and scholarships to cover many school expenses. With the help of state aid, more students are choosing to take advantage of the better academic and extracurricular programs available at prep schools. Contact your regional school board or related school choice programs for more information on financial aid programs. A few of these organizations are listed below:

Center for School Change
Hubert H. Humphrey Institute of Public Affairs
University of Minnesota
301 19th Avenue South
Minneapolis, MN 55455
(612) 626-1834

Choice in Education Foundation, Inc.
365 South Griggs Midway Building
1821 University Avenue West
St. Paul, MN 55401-2801
(612) 644-8547

Coalition for Educational Choice
43K Stoney Run
Maple Shade, NJ 08052
(609) 742-1170

The Manhattan Institute/Center for Education Innovation
52 Vanderbilt Avenue
New York, NY 10017
(212) 599-7000

Partners Advancing Values in Education (PAVE)
1434 West State Street
Milwaukee, WI 53233
(414) 342-1505

For additional information on private and alternative schools contact the National Association of Independent Schools Access Hotline at (800) 343-9138; the Boarding Schools Answerline at (800) 541-5908; or one of the following organizations:

The Association of Boarding Schools
1620 L Street, NW
Washington, DC 20036
(800) 541-5908

The Federation of American and International Schools
1620 L Street, NW
Washington, DC 20036

International Coalition of Boys' Schools
c/o Dr. Richard Hawley
2785 S. O. M. Center Road
Hunting Valley, OH 44022
(216) 831-2200

Junior Boarding Schools
c/o Tom Army
528 Pomfret Street
Pomfret, CT 06258

National Association of Independent Schools (NAIS)
1620 L Street, NW
Washington, DC 20036
(202) 973-9700

National Coalition of Girls' Schools
228 Main Street
Concord, MA 01742
(508) 287-4485

Programs Assisting Minority Students:

A Better Chance
419 Boylston Street
Boston, MA 02116
(617) 421-0950

American Indian Science and Engineering Society (AISES)
1630 30th Street, Suite 301
Boulder, CO 80301-1014
(303) 939-0023

ASPIRA of America, Inc.
1112 16th Street, NW, Suite 340
Washington, DC 20036
(202) 835-3600
(For Latino youth)

You can also write to NAIS for a copy of their guide *Choosing the Right School*. This guide provides information and advice on school selection, school visits and interviews, the admissions process, and school costs. The guide is also available online at http://www.schools.com:80/nais/pub/choosing/right-school.html. For information on financial aid for private schools request the free guide *Financial Aid at Elementary and Secondary Schools* from NAIS.

HOME SCHOOLING

Thousands of parents across the country choose to educate their children outside of the traditional school structure. Reasons for home schooling include inadequate local schools, religious beliefs, and an attempt to better serve children who would thrive in a more personal environment. Some parents do all the teaching themselves, while others join a network of home-schooling families. Home-schooling curricula can include trips to museums, volunteering, and extensive research projects, as well as more traditional lessons. Also, some home-schooled students participate in athletic or other extracurricular activities through their local high schools.

There are plenty of opportunities to seek out challenging and varied programs to meet your academic interests and requirements. However, it's up to your child to seek them out. Finding the right program for him can make the difference between snoring through dull classes and learning what really interests him.

"If there were one thing I could suggest to parents to help their children succeed, it would be to teach them to take responsibility for their actions. Then everything else, including academics, will fall into place."

—High school guidance counselor

25

SUMMARY

To build a challenging study plan that will meet both admissions requirements and your teenager's needs for interesting courses, her choices lie both within your local high school and outside of it. From local AP and IB programs to magnet schools, summer programs, and prep schools, there are many options available for students looking to get the most out of their high school years. Building a study plan will help your child get on the path to enjoying high school while preparing to get into the college she wants.

We've included some tracking sheets to help you and your child start a study plan. On the next page is a sample study plan to guide you. (This schedule assumes the student takes 6 classes per semester, not including physical and health education.)

This is just one example of a study plan. There are thousands of potentially effective study plans, one or more of which is right for your child. Help him develop his own unique plan, letting his requirements, interests, and the availability of classes and special programs guide you.

Visit Kaplan's Web site, www.kaplan.com/downloads/ for a year-end tracking sheet to help you and your son or daughter look back at the year's classes and plan for the coming term. You'll also find a helpful quiz about preparing for college.

TELL YOUR TEEN

* Build a study plan early to allow you to consider alternative programs.
* Don't forget to consider college admissions requirements.
* Take advanced classes in at least two subject areas.

SAMPLE STUDY PLAN

Freshman Year

Subject	First Semester	Second Semester
English	Composition I	Composition II
Social Studies	American Studies I	American Studies II
Mathematics	Algebra I	Algebra II
Sciences	Biology I	Biology II
Foreign Language	Latin I	Latin II
Art and Music	None	None
Business Ed.	Typing I	Typing I
Physical Ed.	Basic Phys. Ed. I	Basic Phys. Ed. II

Sophomore Year

Subject	First Semester	Second Semester
English	Advanced Composition	Research Techniques
Social Studies	Immigration in the U.S.	Anthropology
Mathematics	Advanced Algebra I	Advanced Algebra II
	Geometry	Geometry
Sciences	Advanced Biology	Advanced Biology
Foreign Language	Spanish I	Spanish I
Art and Music	None	None
Business Ed.	Computer Science I	Computer Science II
Phys. Ed.	Tennis I	Tennis II

Junior Year

Subject	First Semester	Second Semester
English	American Literature I	American Lit. II
Social Studies	European Studies	World Politics
Mathematics	Trigonometry I	Trigonometry II
Sciences	Chemistry I	Chemistry II
Foreign Language	Spanish III	Spanish IV
Art and Music	Percussion I	Percussion II
Business Ed.	None	None
Phys. Ed.	Health Education I	Swimming I

Senior Year

Subject	First Semester	Second Semester
English	English Literature I	English Literature II
Social Studies	Psychology	Sociology
Mathematics	Calculus	Calculus
Sciences	Physics I	Physics II
Foreign Language	Spanish V	Spanish VI
Art and Music	Art History I	Art History II
Business Ed.	None	None
Phys. Ed.	Basic Phys. Ed. III	Basic Phys. Ed. IV

INTERNET RESOURCES

Alternative Programs and Schools

International Baccalaureate. http://www.ibo.org
Information about the International Baccalaureate program including a history of the program, a detailed course curriculum, and listing of offices and staff.

National Coalition of Girls' Schools. http://www.ncgs.org
Directory of schools and description of publications.

Online Boarding School Directory. http://www.schools.com
Sponsored by the Federation of American International Schools (FAIS) and the Association of Boarding Schools (TABS). Preview school catalogs, photographs, and application and admissions procedures along with a search application that lets you match your criteria to hundreds of schools.

Independent-Study and Other Online Long-Distance Learning Programs

Barrington U. http://www.barrington.edu
Specializes in distance learning, home study, correspondence, independent study, and adult education.

Chrysalis School. http://www.chrysalis-school.com
An independent-study program for students of all ages.

CyberEd. http://www.umassd.edu/cybered/distlearninghome.html
U Mass—Dartmouth Division of Continuing Education's online program offers accredited college courses to anyone, anywhere.

Cyber High School. http://www.cyberhigh.org
A private, online, college preparatory school. Instruction takes place over the Internet using curriculum specifically designed for students who are motivated to work independently.

Distance Learning Resource Network. http:www.wested.org/tie/dlrn
Links to dozens of distance learning programs, plus other resources.

Indiana U—Bloomington, Division of Extended Studies.
http://www.extend.indiana.edu
High school and college courses.

Knowledge Online™. http://www.meu.edu
Information on home-study courses in the Web and in video.

Novanet. http://www.nn.com
Computer-based materials in over 150 subject areas.

U. of Missouri Center for Independent Study.
http://indepstudy.ext.missouri.edu/
University and continuing-education, home-study courses via computer.

U. of Wisconsin, Independent Learning. http://www.uwex.edu/ilearn/
Nearly 600 correspondence courses for credit.

Programs for Gifted Students

The Center for Talent Development, Northwestern University (CTD).
http://ctdnet.acns.nwu.edu/
Descriptions of CTD course offerings for gifted students, online articles, access to
the CTD virtual community, and more.

The Center for Excellence in Education. http://rsi.cee.org/
Listings of jobs, internships, and programs offered.

The Center for Talented Youth (CTY), Johns Hopkins University.
http://www.jhu.edu/~gifted
Program opportunities, publications, and center home pages.

Education Program for Gifted Youth (EPGY).
http://http:www-epgy.stanford.edu
Information on Stanford University's offerings for its talented students.

TIP, The Talent Identification Program, Duke University.
http://www.tip.duke.edu/
TIP's home page, with information on research educational opportunities.

Home Schooling

Home School Legal Defense Association. http://www.hslda.org
Summaries of state home-schooling laws.

National Home Education Research Institute. http://www.nheri.org
A research clearinghouse on home-schooling issues.

Home Education. http://www.home-ed-magazine.com
A home-schooling magazine.

Kaleidoscapes. http://www.kaleidoscapes.com
Bulletin boards and info for home schoolers.

School is Dead: Learn in Freedom! http://www.learninfreedom.org
Lists colleges that accept home schoolers.

Academic Summer Programs

Barnard College. http://www.barnard.columbia.edu
E-mail to: pcp@barnard.columbia.edu

Brown U. http://www.brown.edu
E-mail to: summer_studies@brown.edu

George Washington U. http://www.gwu.edu
E-mail to: sumprogs@gwis2.circ.gwu.edu

Harvard Summer School. http://dcewww.harvard.edu/summer/

New York University. http://www.nyu.edu/summer

Philadelphia U. of the Arts. E-mail to: pcuarts@netaxs.com

Smith College. http://www.smith.edu/
E-mail to: gscordilis@smith.smith.edu (science program),
or rhosmer@smith.smith.edu (arts and humanities program).

Stanford Summer Session.
http://www.leland.stanford.edu/dept/csss/summer/courses.html
E-mail to: summer.session@forsythe.stanford.edu

SUNY at Potsdam. http://www.potsdam.edu/cont.ed/summer.camps.html

U. of Pennsylvania. http://www.sas.upenn.edu/cgs/cgs.Programs.youth/
E-mail to: shale@sas.upenn.edu

Tracking Sheet 1.1

HIGH SCHOOL REQUIREMENTS

Subject	Minimum Years of Study	Classes
English		
Mathematics		
Science		
Social Studies		
Foreign Language		
Art and Music		
Other:		
_____		
_____		
_____		
_____		
_____		

Tracking Sheet 1.2

COLLEGE ADMISSIONS REQUIREMENTS

Subject	Minimum Years of Study	Classes
English		
Mathematics		
Science		
Social Studies		
Foreign Language		
Art and Music		
Other:		
_____		
_____		
_____		
_____		

Tracking Sheet 1.3

CONSOLIDATED REQUIREMENTS

Subject	Minimum Years of Study	Classes
English		
Mathematics		
Science		
Social Studies		
Foreign Language		
Art and Music		
Other:		
_____		
_____		
_____		
_____		
_____		

Tracking Sheet 1.4

STUDY PLAN (PAGE 1 OF 4)
Freshman Year

Subject	First Semester	Second Semester	Subject	First Semester	Second Semester
English			Physical Education		
Social Studies			Other:		
Mathematics			Other:		
Sciences			Other:		
Foreign Language					
Art and Music					

Tracking Sheet 1.4

STUDY PLAN (PAGE 2 OF 4)
Sophomore Year

Subject	First Semester	Second Semester	Subject	First Semester	Second Semester
English			Physical Education		
Social Studies			Other:		
Mathematics			Other:		
Sciences			Other:		
Foreign Language					
Art and Music					

Tracking Sheet 1.4

STUDY PLAN (PAGE 3 OF 4)
Junior Year

Subject	First Semester	Second Semester	Subject	First Semester	Second Semester
English			Physical Education		
Social Studies			Other:		
Mathematics			Other:		
Sciences			Other:		
Foreign Language					
Art and Music					

Tracking Sheet 1.4

STUDY PLAN (PAGE 4 OF 4)
Senior Year

Subject	First Semester	Second Semester	Subject	First Semester	Second Semester
English			Physical Education		
Social Studies			Other:		
Mathematics			Other:		
Sciences			Other:		
Foreign Language					
Art and Music					

CHAPTER 2

Grades

WHAT STUDENTS ASK

- **What can I do to get better grades?**
- **How do high school grades affect college admissions?**
- **What honors might I be awarded?**

Is your child obsessed with grades? Does he track his average with every quiz, exam, and report card? Join the club. Most college-bound students worry about their grades until they're accepted in college, and for good reason. While his choice of classes reveals his interests and motivation, grades show how successful he is at meeting the challenges set before him.

How important are grades? Very! In addition to showing performance, grades also determine class rank and standing, eligibility for advanced classes, honors, and scholarships, and likelihood of admission into colleges and special programs.

There are several key statistics, based on grades, that you and your child can use to figure out how well he's doing in school. These stats include the grade point average, the cumulative grade point average, area averages, class rank, and percentile standing.

GRADE POINT AVERAGE

Grade point average includes all of the classes taken for credit each academic year. Here's one example.

FRESHMAN YEAR GRADES—AN EXAMPLE

Course	Semester 1	Semester 2
Algebra I & II	88	91
Biology I & II	85	88
American Studies I & II	95	93
Latin I & II	80	80
Basic Comp. I & II	90	90
Typing I & II	85	85
Physical Education I & II*	80	80

*Physical education and other nonacademic courses are typically excluded from the GPA and other grade-based statistics.

This student received a first-semester average of 87.2 and a second-semester average of 87.8 for a freshman grade point average of 87.5. Though her average doesn't show huge improvement, it shows some, which is important—each subsequent semester's grades should be higher. A higher second-semester average suggests that you can handle more difficult work and get higher grades. Your goal should be to achieve a higher average with each passing semester and academic year.

CUMULATIVE GRADE POINT AVERAGE

The cumulative grade point average—often called the GPA—is the average of all of the high school courses you've taken to date. The GPA is calculated by adding together all of your academic grades and dividing that total by the number of courses taken. Notice that after the first semester of your sophomore year, your cumulative GPA won't be the same as your GPA. Here's an example:

SOPHOMORE YEAR GRADES—AN EXAMPLE		
Course	Semester 1	Semester 2
Advanced Algebra I & II	90	90
Geometry I & II	87	92
Advanced Biology I & II	90	92
Advanced Composition	85	
Research Techniques		87
Spanish I & II	93	95
Immigration	98	
Anthropology		94
Tennis I & II*	83	85

*Not included in average

This student achieved an 90.5 average in the first semester of the sophomore year (the sum of grades for advanced algebra plus geometry plus advanced biology plus advanced composition plus Spanish plus immigration, divided by six). Her second-semester average is 91.7, for a GPA of 91.1 (calculated by taking the sum of the first semester total plus second semester total, divided by 12) and a cumulative GPA of 89.2 (calculated by taking the sum of all courses taken in high school and dividing by the number of courses taken). Since your goal is to increase your GPA with each passing semester, this student is well on her way to achieving that goal. For the first four semesters, our sample student's GPA goes from an 87.2 to an 87.8 to a 90.5, then to a 91.7. Note that she is receiving higher grades in more challenging courses. As a freshman she took algebra, biology, and basic composition. As a sophomore she added the more challenging courses of advanced algebra, advanced biology, and advanced composition.

AREA AVERAGE

Colleges want to be sure that a student has mastered the basics before she graduates from high school. Since the main subject areas provide the material for learning and developing these skills, they track the averages in these areas. Area averages are calculated for the following subjects:

- English
- Mathematics
- Sciences
- Social Studies
- Foreign Languages
- Fine/Musical Arts

AREA AVERAGE BY SUBJECT AREA An Example		
Subject: Science	**Freshman Year**	**Sophomore Year**
Biology I	85	
Biology II	88	
Adv. Biology I		85
Adv. Biology II		90

To determine the area average in science after two years of study, you would sum the two semesters of biology and advanced biology grades and divide this total by four. The science average after two years is an 87. This average represents an improvement over the freshman science area average of 86.5. This improvement suggests that this student is mastering basic science skills.

Tracking area averages can help a student better understand her strengths and weaknesses by subject area. Area averages in the high 80's and 90's suggest that you like and do well in an area, while averages below 80 may suggests that you dislike or have not yet mastered that subject area. Good and improving averages in the key academic areas is often the evidence that many admissions officers look for to determine your readiness to tackle college courses. In which subjects does your daughter have the highest area averages? The lowest? How does this compare to her subject interests? As you answer these questions, you should begin to see a pattern suggesting her likes, dislikes, strengths, and weaknesses.

CLASS RANK

Class rank shows your child's standing relative to other students at her school and in her grade. Ranking is done by cumulative grade point average. The student with the highest average is ranked number one. This ranking continues, in descending order, until the student with the lowest cumulative average is reached.

Class rank is a favorite statistic for admissions committees since it provides a clear indication of place in the class. It helps to answer the question of how one measures up against one's classmates, all of whom have been subjected to the same curriculum, teachers, and grading system. The higher your rank (e.g., number 5 instead of 50 in a class of 100 students), the more impressive your performance is thought to be. What is your child's class rank? She should actively look to improve her ranking in high school over time, by improving grades.

PERCENTILE STANDING

Percentile standing is calculated as class rank divided by the size of the class. It is often used as a substitute statistic for class rank by admissions committees. Standing is often discussed in the following terms:

- Top twentieth—top 5 percent of the class
- Top tenth—top 10 percent of the class
- Top quartile—top 25 percent of the class
- Top half—top 50 percent of the class

What is your child's class standing? Has she made progress since her freshman year?

In many highly selective colleges and universities, the overwhelming majority of entering students graduate in the top 25 percent of their high school class. If your child's target schools include the very selective colleges, he may want to make getting child's into the top 10–25 percent of his class a high priority.

You will see some of these grade-based statistics on your child's report card and transcript. Check them to be sure you understand what they are and how they are computed. If the statistics are not listed on the report card, ask your child's counselor how you can go about getting them; or you may need to calculate them yourself.

COLLEGES AND UNIVERSITIES WITH MORE THAN 50% OF ENTERING FRESHMAN COMING FROM THE TOP 10% OF THEIR HIGH SCHOOL CLASS
Examples by State

AL: Birmingham-Southern

CA: California Institute of Technology
Claremont McKenna
Harvey Mudd
Pepperdine
Pomona
Stanford
U. of California at Berkeley, Irvine, Los Angeles, Riverside, San Diego, Santa Barbara, and Santa Cruz

CO: Colorado School of Mines

CT: U.S. Coast Guard Academy
Wesleyan
Yale

DC: Georgetown

FL: U. of Florida

GA: Emory
Georgia Institute of Technology

IA: Grinnell

IL: Northwestern
U. of Chicago

IN: Rose-Hulman Institute of Technology
U. of Notre Dame

MA: Amherst
Boston College
College of the Holy Cross
Harvard
Massachusetts Institute of Technology
Tufts
Wellesley
Williams

MD: Johns Hopkins

ME: Bowdoin
Colby

MI: U. of Michigan—Ann Arbor

MN: Carleton

MO: Washington

NC: Davidson
Duke
U. of North Carolina at Chapel Hill
Wake Forest

NH: Dartmouth

NJ: Princeton

NY: Columbia
Cooper Union
Cornell
NYU
Polytechnic U.
U.S. Military Academy

OH: Case Western Reserve

PA: Bryn Mawr
Carnegie Mellon
Haverford
Swarthmore
U. of Pennsylvania

RI: Brown

TN: Vanderbilt

TX: Rice
Trinity

UT: Brigham Young

VA: College of William and Mary
U. of Virginia
Washington and Lee

VT: Middlebury

GOALS AND GRADES

When college admissions officers are asked what they look for in grades, they often respond:

1. Consistency, if not improvement, in grades over time
2. Good averages in key academic areas (e.g., math, English and science)
3. Good grades in the student's area(s) of interest

Consistency and Improvement

Grades are often thought to be an accurate measure of your academic ability. If you consistently achieve grades of B or better, admissions officers may conclude that you are a good student with the ability to consistently achieve a grade level of B or better at their school. Here, an "A" student is thought to be "excellent," a "B" student is "good," a "C" student is "fair," and a "D" student would be considered "poor." If your child is aiming for a competitive college or program, he'll want to shoot for grades that are consistently in the B and better range.

What colleges and universities like to see, even more than consistency, is improvement in grades throughout high school. This is true no matter what the starting level. This improvement suggests an increased interest in and application to your studies over time. That colleges look for improving grades is good news for most students, since it gives them something to shoot for while also allowing them to recover from mediocre performance during early years in high school.

Area of Interest

Let's say your daughter want to become a doctor. There's just one glitch: Her area averages in math and science are the lowest on her report card. In fact, they are in the low 70's, while her area averages in English, social studies, languages, and the arts are all in the upper 80's or low 90's. What message does this send to an admissions committee? That she does not know her own strengths and weaknesses. Or is it that she doesn't have realistic career objectives? Admissions committees make the very reasonable assumption that students perform better in those subjects that interest them. This makes sense: If a subject excites you, you will probably spend more time on it. If you spend more time studying it, your understanding of that topic should increase and translate into a higher grade. So encourage your child to review his area averages and ask himself if he is performing better in those areas that:

- He thinks that he has an interest in
- The college program that he'd like to apply to requires
- The career he thinks he's like to pursue requires

If he is not performing as well in his areas of interest as he is in the rest of his high school program, ask yourself, why not? Is he really interested in that subject? His grades provide a window to his interests; examine the view. This is the window that admissions officers will be looking through. Your son should project an image of self-awareness and rationality to admissions committees. Having his grades support his declared interests is one way to provide a supporting view. Evaluate his grade performance by area of interest over time by recording his grades and the relevant statistics. Use these statistics to help you track progress against goals (e.g., increasing averages over time) and to check your assumptions about strengths and weaknesses (e.g., higher area averages in those areas of interest to him).

STUDY SKILLS

Good grades aren't only the key to getting into the college of your choice. They also represent the building blocks for mastery of difficult subjects and critical-thinking and learning skills. How do you improve grades over time? Typically, great grades begin with solid study skills. Master these skills and you're likely to see higher grades.

In a nutshell, study skills are the methods you apply when learning. They include how you approach your work, set goals, plan your activities, and approach your life (since life itself is probably your biggest exercise in learning). Let's discuss some study skills your child can use to improve his grades.

The Approach

How your teen approaches work is everything. Does she generally have a great attitude and look forward to learning each day? Does she set clear and achievable goals for herself? Having a positive attitude with attainable goals are the keys to approaching her work for success. How do you establish an effective approach for learning that will increase your chances of getting better grades? Encourage your child to try to use the following ideas when she is in the classroom and outside of it.

An Effective Approach to Learning

Maintain a positive, "can do" attitude. Every time you face a new activity tell yourself:

- I can do it.
- It will be easy.
- It will be fun.
- I will learn something new.
- What I learn will make me stronger and smarter.

When you approach each opportunity to learn with this kind of enthusiasm and confidence, you are choosing to view learning as an exciting adventure. Adopting this positive approach to learning is more than half the battle to mastering effective study skills. Just think about it. If every time you entered a new learning situation you knew you would have fun, get a lot out of it, and that it would be easy, wouldn't you jump at every opportunity to learn? Of course. Maintaining a positive attitude and telling yourself that "it will be easy and fun" instead of "it will be hard and boring" will change the way you approach learning for the better. Remember, the more you enjoy something, the more time you'll to spend with it. When students apply this to studies, their grades often will improve.

Setting Goals

One great thing about grades is that you can use them to set clear and attainable goals for yourself. You can say, for example, that next semester you will get a "B+" instead of a "B" in biology. This gives you something clear to shoot for. Most of us need not just something to shoot for, but also a reason to go after it. Motivation plays a huge role in getting us to do things. This motivation can be positive ("I want higher grades") or negative ("lower grades will keep me out of my target school"). When you set goals for yourself, always provide the incentive—the "why" you should go after them. This will come in handy during the middle of the semester or on weekends when you are saying to yourself, "why bother with my studies?"

"Never lose focus of your goals. In my freshman year, I decided that I wanted to be recognized as one of the top ten in my class. I kept that goal in mind throughout high school to help motivate me."

—High school senior, ranked in top 10 of graduating class

Goals help you to clearly define what you want, when you want it, and why it is important for you to get it. A clear set of goals provide the direction and focus you need to channel your energy towards achieving what you want. Goal setting also keeps you from spending a lot of time on activities that will not deliver results. All this said, how can you help your child come up with goals that provide him with both concrete objectives and a clear sense of direction? Advise him to follow these steps:

Step 1: Write down what you want. Be as clear as possible (e.g., "I want at least a "B" in all of my classes this term.")

Step 2: Make sure that they are attainable. There's nothing like shooting for goals that you cannot make (e.g., "I want all 100's by the end of the semester" when you are already midway through the semester and have averages in the mid-80's).

Step 3: Go after your goals with enthusiasm and a positive attitude. A positive attitude with clear goal setting provides an unbeatable combination for getting better grades.

Planning

Like adults, teens make more progress when they approach work with a plan. Your child should make plans for each activity by the day, week, and/or semester. Her plan should list the activities that she needs to complete as well as the times or dates she needs to complete them by. In drafting an activity plan for each upcoming week, be sure she schedules enough time to easily complete each task, whether it is nightly homework or upcoming an exam. Planning allows students to organize their lives—to complete each activity and goal established more easily and successfully.

STAYING ON TOP

Buy your teen a pocket organizer to help him keep his life organized, or check out electronic or software versions that are available.

REWARDS

A byproduct of getting great grades is receiving recognition and honors for your work. These honors can take the form of school-based awards to national programs.

School-Based Honors

Most high schools recognize students who receive good grades. This recognition can come in several forms:

Honor roll. Semester averages of 85 or better can generally land students on a schoolwide honor roll.

Department lists. Students receiving grades of 90 or better, or receiving the top grade in a class, or maintaining the highest cumulative subject-area average are often recognized for their performance.

Graduation Honors. Students ranking first and second in their class are often designated the Valedictorian and salutatorian of their class. These students receive special recognition and are often asked to address the class during graduation ceremonies.

These are just some of the many ways individual high schools recognize outstanding students during the school year and throughout each student's high school career. Your child's guidance counselor can probably tell you other ways excellence in academics is recognized at her school. Competing for recognition is another way to provide yourself with ongoing incentives to help you provide the "why" to getting and maintaining great grades.

National Honors

Students with solid academic records can also qualify for national honors programs. The most well known of these programs is the National Honor Society (NHS), an organization that recognizes the outstanding performance of high school students. The NHS was founded in 1921 to serve as a national honor roll for students demonstrating a level of excellence in the areas of scholarship, leadership, service, and character. Each year, students at more than 15,000 schools across the country qualify for the NHS and participate in its membership activities. Most high schools sponsor a local chapter of the NHS. Any student in the tenth through twelfth grades is eligible for membership, provided he or she meets the selection criteria, the most basic of which is scholarship. To qualify for membership in the NHS, a student must have a minimum cumulative GPA of 85/B/3.0. Each school is also able to set a higher GPA requirement for admission into its local chapter.

Grades are often the only objective criteria clearly stated for membership for most chapters. The other criteria—service, leadership, and character—are more subjective and can vary widely from one chapter to the next.

All members of NHS receive certificates of membership when they are inducted into the organization. Once you are a member of the NHS you also become eligible to participate in its programs, including:

- NHS National Conference which is held over a weekend each year. This motivational conference features national speakers and is attended by NHS members from around the country.
- The NHS scholarship competition that annually awards 250 scholarships of $1,000 each to NHS seniors.
- The six-day NHS Leadership Camps are held around the country to train members to be better leaders.

For more information about the National Honor Society, contact your child's school's NHS advisor or the guidance office. If it does not have a chapter, you can contact the NHS for more information at: National Association of Secondary School Principals, Department of Student Activities, 1904 Association Drive, Reston, VA 22091-1537; phone (703) 860-0200; fax (703) 476-5432; or e-mail at nhs/njhs@nassp.org.

In 1995, another national honor society for high school students was formed. The American Technology Honor Society (ATHS) was established by the National Association of Secondary School Principals (NASSP) and the Technology Students Association (TSA) to recognize students demonstrating outstanding skills in the area of technology. For more information on ATHS member schools and programs, contact: ATHS, 1904 Association Drive, Reston, VA 22091; phone (703) 860-0200; or e-mail at aths@nassp.org.

There are additional honors programs and awards you can qualify for if you are consistently receiving great grades. Some are administered through programs for gifted students, listed in chapter one. There are also programs sponsored by organizations like the United States Department of Energy (DOE). The DOE Honors Program runs for two weeks each summer, accepting six outstanding students from each state; participants are placed in DOE laboratories to do research. For more information about this program, contact: Technology Training Programs, Division of Educational Programs, Argonne National Laboratory, Argonne, IL 60439-4845; or call them at(630) 252-3366. You should also discuss this and other opportunities with your guidance office.

SUMMARY

If your child successfully integrates study skills into his daily life—a positive attitude, clear and attainable goals, and daily planning—he'll find that he will be more confident and in control of his learning. The reward for mastering these study skills will be higher grades. Furthermore, recording grade statistics will help him to keep himself on track to meeting his goals. Help him decide what grade level you both believe he can reach and maintain at school. Work to reach that level; then, beat it! Your child should constantly push himself to do better despite the increased challenge of the coursework. Hit an acceptable grade level, achieve consistency, then strive for progress. This is what colleges expect.

Review your child's progress each year. This includes re-evaluating strengths and weaknesses by subject area. Of course, one of the greatest rewards of getting good grades is the personal satisfaction of a job well done. (Still, receiving honors and awards based on your achievements feels mighty good as well.) Remember, consistent and strong grade performance across the board, and particularly in areas of interest, can provide the incentive your child needs to achieve her goals—the biggest of which is acceptance into the college of choice.

> "If there were one thing I could suggest to high school students to succeed academically, it would be to read, read, read!"
>
> —High school
> guidance counselor

TELL YOUR TEEN

- Target, reach and then maintain an acceptable grade level.
- Improve your grade performance over time.
- Seek out recognition for your outstanding academic performance.

INTERNET RESOURCES

Academic Resources:

AskERIC. http://ericir.syr.edu/
Online virtual library of subject-based lesson plans, databases, and related subject-based materials.

CollegeNET. http://www.collegenet.com
Includes a directory of links to academic resources, including foreign language dictionaries.

CCCnet. http://www.cccnet.com
A place to learn and polish reading, writing, social science, math, and science skills.

Eisenhower National Clearinghouse (ENC). http://www.enc.org/
Lessons and activities in math and science.

Foreign Languages Resources.
http://www.itp.berkeley.edu/~thorne/humanresources
A list of foreign language/culture sites on the Web, via UC Berkeley.

The Human-Languages Page.
http://www.willamette.edu/~tjones/language-page.html
A site devoted to bringing together information about the languages of the world from dictionaries, to language tutorials, to spoken samples of languages.

Lecture on Academic Honesty. http://ac.grin.edu/~hunterj/achon/lecture.html
Want to know more about the rules governing when to cite sources and how in your assignments to best avoid charges of plagiarism? This site reviews these ideas and more.

The MAD Scientist Network. http://www.madsci.org
Fun, with links to loads of science resources, from Washington University Medical School.

MegaMath. http://www.c3.lanl.gov/mega-math
Source of challenging math problems. Games and lots of other problem solving math exercises.

Researchpaper.com. http://www.researchpaper.com
Ideas for research papers, plus advice on using the Internet for school papers.

Student Guide.
http://www.byu.edu/acd1/ed/insci/projects/wwwsubjectguide.html
A guide to databases, lesson plans, activities, exhibits, museums, and online directories, by academic subject area.

Syndicate.Com. http://syndicate.com
Vocabulary word puzzles from daily newspapers, a notebook to help students write better essays and term papers, and a vocabulary comic strip are featured on this site.

wave. http://gauss.uni.uiuc.edu/
Tutorials and notebooks available in many high school math subjects including algebra, calculus, geometry, trigonometry, and statistics.

Homework Helpers

"Ask-A" services allow you to pose questions to professionals.

Ask the Astronomer. http://umbra.nascom.nasa.gov/spartan/ask-astronomers
Courtesy of NASA.

Ask a Chemist. http://www.flinet.com/~gurumo.question.html
Brought to you by Dr. Science.

Ask Dr. Science. http://www.drscience.com
The radio personality who "knows more than you do." Light and funny, but with links to real experts.

Ask an Engineer. http://www.city-net.com/~tombates/askengalt.html

Ask an Expert (scientist). http://sln.fi.edu/tfi/publications/askexprt.html

Ask a Geologist. http://walrus.wr.usgs.gov/docs/ask-a-ge.html

Electronic Library. http://www.elibrary.com
Research service with searchable access to hundreds of newspaper, magazines, books, and photographs for a monthly fee.

Ask Dr. Math. http://forum.swarthmore.edu/dr.math/dr-math.html
Service offers monthly and weekly math programs. You can e-mail your math questions, or search their archives; high school student math mentor program also available.

Kid's Web. http://www.npac.syr.edu/textbook/kidsweb
Digital library to help students with homework and research projects. Arranged by subject area.

Reed Interactive. http://www.reedbooks.com.au/index.html
Offers study aids for students, including Hot Topics: a guide to current events with suggested study questions and projects.

Scientific American. http://www.sciam.com/askexpert/
The magazine's ask-an-expert site.

University of Michigan Public Library. http://ipl.sils.umich.edu/youth/
An electronic catalog of reference works on the Internet. The Youth section features a librarian who helps with homework questions.

Virtual Writing Laboratory. http://owl.english.purdue.edu.
online writing lab sponsored by Purdue University that allows students to talk with tutors about planning and writing their papers. Also includes useful links to online sources of information for researching and other writing.

Honors Programs

National Honor Society. http://www.nassp.org
Information on the National Honor Society Scholarships plus other programs from the National Association of Secondary School Principals.

Reference Desk

Library of Congress. http://www.loc.gov/
View digitized historical collections and visit library reading room complete with U.S. and foreign newspapers, books, and government documents.

Map Viewer. http://pubweb.parc.xerox.com/map
See map images from areas around the globe.

National Archives. http://www.nara.gov/
The WWW site of the National Archives and Records Administration (NARA). Search the historical records of the three branches of government (executive, legislative, and judicial).

Project Gutenberg. http://www.gutenberg.net
Full electronic texts of fictional and non-fictional works, including fairy tales, the Bible, Shakespeare, and reference titles (Roget's Thesaurus, almanacs, encyclopedias, and dictionaries).

Study Skills

Study Skills. http://plan.educ.indiana.edu/
Library of materials for improving study skills. Covers topics like getting better grades, improving your memory, and how to write well.

Study Skills Self-Help Information. http://www.ucc.vt.edu/stdysk/stdyhlp.html
Provided by Virginia Tech's Counseling Center. Suggestions for scheduling your time; a study skills checklist; and, tips on editing class notes.

CHAPTER 3

Exams

WHAT STUDENTS ASK

- **When should I take each of the standardized tests?**
- **Should I take the SAT or ACT?**
- **How can I earn college credit while I'm still in high school?**

Exam: It's every student's least favorite four-letter word. While your child has probably taken hundreds of tests over the past ten years or so, how she takes tests, and which tests she takes, have more impact now than ever on getting into the college of her dreams.

There are two types of college admissions tests taken in high school—standardized and content-based exams. Standardized tests are designed to test knowledge and skills gained over time, like vocabulary, critical reading, thinking, and problem solving. The scores on these exams often determine eligibility for college admissions and scholarships. In contrast, content-based exams test knowledge of specific subject areas like biology or French. The scores on these exams also determine college admission, as well as placement in college courses. In this chapter, we'll focus on the exams that are most often requested by U.S. colleges and universities for admission—what they are, what they test, when is the best time to take them, and how often they should be taken.

The most widely taken standardized tests are the College Entrance Examination Board's PSAT and SAT I, and the American College Testing Company's ACT. These exams test acquired learning, particularly vocabulary, reading, and math skills. The PSAT, like the SAT I, does not directly test subject matter covered in nonmath high school courses. The ACT, however, does attempt to test some of the subject matter in your child's study plan.

Why do colleges require prospective students to take these tests? The rationale is that these tests create a standard against which all students can measure up. High school education varies widely in the United States; the mix of schools include expensive and exclusive preparatory schools, overcrowded and underfunded inner-city schools, rural and suburban schools, and religious and nonsectarian schools. There are also significant differences in classes offered, grading, and teacher quality. There is no easy way to compare the 90 average of a student attending a specialized, inner-city high school with that of a student in a New England preparatory school or a Midwestern parochial school. Colleges and universities consider these tests to be the great equalizer. This is one exam that most college-bound students will take regardless of school type, geography, and family income. Most college applicants, in a given year, will take these exams on one of a handful of test dates (most often in the fall and spring of the junior year or fall of the senior year). Many colleges also believe that the results from these tests are strong predictors of college performance. Finally, these tests force high schools to adopt similar course requirements for college-bound students. By adopting similar graduation requirements, this is one of the few ways high schools can be sure that their students will be academically prepared for college. So, by forcing high schools and their students to focus on these admissions tests, the colleges that require them acquire a set of data to evaluate candidates who come from vastly different high school backgrounds.

THE PSAT/NMSQT

The Preliminary SAT/National Merit Scholarship Qualifying Test (PSAT/NMSQT) is an exam given once a year, in October, mostly to juniors and sophomores. This test serves a dual purpose: It's a practice test for the SAT I, and it's a qualifying exam for the selection of National Merit Scholars. Each year more than one million students take the PSAT. They receive an introduction to the content and question types that appear on the SAT I. PSAT scores are not reported to colleges, so you can take the test without fear that your score will affect your chances for admission.

Taking the PSAT

The PSAT is two hours long and has two parts: math and verbal. The math section tests your ability to solve problems and make quantitative comparisons between equations and numbers. The PSAT is also designed to test your grasp of the basic principles of arithmetic, algebra, and geometry. The best way to prepare for the math section of the PSAT is for your child to include a challenging pre-college math program (at least through geometry) in her study plan and to review the basic principles of these subjects before test day.

> **BRING YOUR CALCULATOR**
>
> Make sure your child brings a calculator with which she's familiar to the PSAT. Students using a calculator, on average, score 10 to 20 points higher on the math section than those who don't.

The verbal section of the PSAT tests vocabulary, thinking, and reading skills. The best way to prepare for this section is to read actively and work diligently to build your vocabulary while in high school. Your child can begin to do this by reading books, newspapers, and magazines. She should also get a note pad to carry with her and jot down words that she comes across, but doesn't know. Encourage her to look these words up. Then, try to use these words at least once a day for the next week. Finally, at the end of the week, encourage her to test herself on the spelling, pronunciation, and definition of the words that she entered in her notebook during that week. Doing this throughout high school helps develop vocabulary skills and will likely result in a higher score on the PSAT's verbal section.

PSAT Scoring

Students receive a verbal and math score, each on a scale from 20 to 80. With the PSAT score report, sent the following December, comes the College Board guide, *About Your PSAT/NMSQT Score.* This bulletin, along with the test book, will help you and your child to understand her scores and performance on the PSAT.

When to Take the PSAT

If at all possible, your child should take the exam for the first time as a sophomore. This gives him risk-free exposure to the exam's format, question types, and content. He can use this practice run to determine where his score is relative to the SAT I scores achieved by students attending the colleges of interest to him. If his scores are low, compared to the college averages, he may want to begin formal preparation for the PSAT and SAT I. Since the exam is designed to test skills acquired over a period of time, early preparation is often the only way to see a significant increase in test scores.

For more information on the PSAT/NMSQT, ask your child's guidance office for the College Board's *PSAT/NMSQT Student Bulletin.* The booklet provides information on test dates, test-taking tips, sample questions, strategies for each question type, a practice test with answers, and information on scholarship programs. You may also want to contact PSAT/NMSQT, P.O. Box 6720, Princeton, N. J. 08541-6720; phone (609) 771-7300 or 7070 for more information.

THE NATIONAL MERIT SCHOLARSHIP (NMS)

A National Merit Scholarship winner is recognized for scholastic performance; this recognition can come in the form of a financial award for college or a recommendation. The process for qualifying and receiving this award takes more than a year, but it begins with the PSAT. All qualified PSAT test takers are considered for a National Merit Scholarship. The requirements include United States citizenship (or residency leading to citizenship) and enrollment in high school. Although more than 25 percent of the students taking the PSAT in a given year are sophomores, only juniors are eligible to compete for this scholarship.

TOOT YOUR HORN

If your child becomes a NMS semi-finalist or finalist, be sure he lets his target colleges know. Many of the very selective colleges target NMS semifinalists, finalists, and financial award winners in their recruitment efforts.

From the group of eligible test takers, 50,000 students are chosen for some recognition. These juniors have achieved the highest PSAT scores in their state. All states choose students based on the Selection Index, which is a student's PSAT math score plus twice the verbal score (notice the emphasis placed on the verbal score). Students are selected in descending order from the highest index until the state's quota is filled. Each state nominates a fixed number of students each year based on that state's representation of all graduating high school students nationwide. Since some states are more populous than others (e.g., New York and California versus Maine and Alaska), it is harder to receive recognition based on PSAT scores in these larger states. By September of the senior year, 35,000 of the 50,000 students will receive Letters of Commendation. The remaining 15,000 students become semifinalists for National Merit Scholarships. Semifinalists represent less than 1 percent of the graduating seniors in the United States, so this designation represents a significant achievement and honor.

"I didn't know how important the PSAT was for qualifying for National Merit Scholarships, so I didn't prepare and do my best. I really regret that."

—High school senior

NMS semifinalists complete and submit a detailed application that includes their transcript, essays, extracurricular activities, SAT I scores, and letters of recommendation in order to be considered for an award. Approximately 90 percent of the semifinalist become National Merit Scholarship finalists. All winners of scholarships are notified by April of their senior year.

TWENTY COLLEGES AND UNIVERSITIES TYPICALLY ENROLLING THE GREATEST NUMBER OF NATIONAL MERIT SCHOLARS

Baylor	U. of Alabama
Brown	U. of Arizona
Carleton	U. of California—San Diego
Case Western Reserve	U. of Chicago
Florida State	U. of Central Florida
Harvard	U. of Florida
Johns Hopkins	U. of Houston
Ohio State	U. of Pennsylvania
Rice	Vanderbilt
Texas A&M	Virginia Polytechnic Institute

Only 6,500, or roughly half, of NMS finalists actually receive a financial award. In the past, these scholarships have ranged from one-time payments to four-year awards. For more information on the National Merit Scholarship Program, including eligibility requirements, the selection process, awards offered, and participating companies and schools, contact: National Merit Scholarship Corporation, 1560 Sherman Avenue, Suite 200, Evanston, IL 60201-4897; phone (847) 866-5100.

In addition to the National Merit Scholarship, there are other scholarship programs that use PSAT/NMSQT scores to determine eligibility. These programs include:

The National Achievement Scholarship Program for Outstanding Negro Students
1560 Sherman Avenue, Suite 200
Evanston, IL 60201-4897

The National Hispanic Scholar Recognition Program
1717 Massachusetts Avenue NW, Suite 401
Washington, DC 20036-2093

The National Scholarship Service and Fund for Negro Students
965 Martin Luther King, Jr., Drive, NW
Atlanta, GA 30315

Telluride Association
217 West Avenue
Ithaca, NY 14850

The last organization runs a six-week scholarship summer program with seminars in the humanities and social sciences for students after their junior year of high school. Students receiving high scores on the PSAT are sent applications forms in early January provided they checked the box on the test to release their scores to the Telluride Association.

THE SAT I

The SAT I is the most widely requested college admissions test taken by high school students in the United States. The SAT I is given nationally about five times each year, is taken by more than 1.2 million students each year (and by about 90 percent of all students entering four-year colleges and universities), and is accepted by more than 2,500 colleges and universities. The SAT I is three hours long and, like the PSAT, is designed to test math and verbal skills. But while the PSAT is a practice test, the SAT is the real thing.

SAT I Scoring

The SAT I is scored on a scale of 200 to 800 for both the math and verbal sections. For the last several years, the average scores for the SAT I have been about 430 for verbal and 480 for math. Unfortunately, in the past, if you scored a 450 on both math and verbal sections, you would think that you did equally well on each section. In fact, you did better than average in the verbal and below average in the math. To make performance on the SAT I easier to understand, in April 1995 the College Board "recentered" the test, or adjusted the scoring so that the average score for all test takers is 500 for the math and verbal sections. This doesn't mean that students taking the SAT I today are any less intelligent than they were in recent years. Only now, at a glance, students are able to tell whether they performed better or worse than the average test taker.

According to College Board figures, in recent years, fewer than 20 percent of all test takers achieve a math score of 600 or better; fewer than 10 percent of test takers score a 600 or higher on the verbal section. (With the current recentered scores, the cutoff for this kind of superior performance is the mid-600's for each section.) Historically, students with three or more years of high school study in the key subject areas like English, math, science, and social studies, earned the highest scores.

A perfect score on the SAT I is still 1600 (800 each on the math and verbal sections). But getting a perfect score doesn't mean answering each question correctly; in a recent test administration, you could get up to four of the 78 verbal questions and one of the 60 math questions wrong and still get a perfect score. But this doesn't mean that thousands of students score 1600. The test is scaled so that no more than an estimated 0.07 percent of the test takers in a given year will end up with a perfect score. That means about 7 out of every 10,000 test takers will earn a 1600 on the SAT I.

SCHOOLS WITH THE TOP 25 PERCENT OF ENTERING STUDENTS WITH COMBINED SAT I SCORES OF 1400+	
Amherst	Massachusetts Institute of Tech.
Brown	Princeton
California Institute of Technology	Rice
Cooper Union	Stanford
Dartmouth	Swarthmore
Duke	U. of Chicago
Harvard	Williams
Johns Hopkins	Yale

Taking the SAT I

College-bound students usually take the SAT I for the first time during the spring of their junior year (March, May or June). There are several benefits to taking the exam then. First, you've probably covered the content and developed the skills needed to do your best. Second, if you decided to prepare for the SAT I after receiving your PSAT scores, you've probably completed your studies by now. Finally, if there is a problem on test day, or you feel you have not achieved your desired score (and you believe with further preparation you can achieve it), there is still time to repeat the exam in the fall of your senior year while meeting college application deadlines.

How often should students take the SAT I? As a general rule, they should take the exam once. Give your child this advice: Use the PSAT as your practice test. Prepare for the SAT I so you can take it once feeling confident that you will achieve your highest possible score. If you take the test, but feel that your scores do not reflect your true abilities or you need a higher score to qualify for the college(s) of your choice, then take it again. However, if after the second try there is no real change in your scores, don't retake the exam. Repeating the exam without significantly increasing in your scores doesn't help you; it simply convinces an admission's committee that your SAT I scores reflect your true ability. Colleges vary in their approach to multiple SAT scores: Some average the scores, others take the highest scores, and still others use the latest scores. If you are concerned about repeating the exam, contact the colleges and universities that you are considering and ask about their approach to multiple SAT I scores.

Your child will receive her scores about four to six weeks after she takes the exam. Remember, all SAT I scores are kept for an indefinite time period and are reported directly to the colleges that she chooses to receive them. If she takes the exam three times, her SAT I score report will contain three sets of math and verbal scores. Score reports will contain SAT I scores for up to six sittings.

Preparing for the SAT I

Although theoretically you're not supposed to be able to study for the PSAT or SAT I, you can get a higher score if you prepare. The higher score comes from experience and practice with the exam's format and content. Therefore, any preparation for the SAT I should include exposure to the format of the test, including instructions and a clear approach to handling each of the question types; a review of the basic math principles (e.g., arithmetic, algebra, and geometry); verbal exercises to improve vocabulary and reading skills; and practice taking the test to learn to pace yourself and concentrate on quickly identifying right answer choices.

Below are a few basic tips to help students prepare for the PSAT and SAT I:

- Familiarize yourself with the question types before you take the test. You don't want to lose valuable testing time trying to figure out what to do.

- Expect easy questions at the beginning of each set. Within each question type (except critical reading), the questions generally get harder as you go along. This means an "obvious" answer is more likely to be correct on the first question of a section, rather than on the last.

- Don't spend too much time on any one question. All correct answers get the same amount of credit, no matter how hard or easy the questions are. Take a watch with you to help with pacing.

- Mark your answers in the right row on the answer sheet. Be especially careful when you skip questions.

- Choose the best answer. Don't waste time by arguing with the test.

- Do your scratch work in the test booklet. You aren't expected to do all the problem solving in your head. But be sure to transfer your answers to the answer sheet. You won't receive credit for anything written in the test book.

- If you can eliminate even one answer choice, guess. Educated guessing can score you points. But the SAT does have a wrong-answer penalty, so don't guess completely randomly.

- You don't have to answer every question. You can still get a great score and leave a couple of questions blank.

The lesson to take away from these tips: *prepare.* Don't take the exam cold! The SAT I is not an IQ test, and just one additional correct answer on the exam can result in a 8- to 12-point improvement in your score. The best way to prepare is to take a challenging college prep curriculum like the one described in the first chapter. However, there are other ways to maximize your score. As a first step, have your child visit his guidance office and ask for the *Bulletin for the SAT Program*, a publication of the Educational Testing Service. It's free and it explains how the test is organized and scored, includes a practice test with answers, and contains key information on test dates and the registration process. If this booklet is not available, write to: College Board/ATP, P.O. Box 6200, Princeton, NJ 08541-6200; telephone (609) 771-7600. You can also call ETS in New Jersey at (609) 921-9000, or in California at (510) 654-1200.

There are other options for test prep. Some high schools provide P/SAT review courses. Check with your child's guidance counselor to see if they are available at her school. Local bookstores carry books and software that contain both content review and practice tests. The College Board, the makers of the PSAT and SAT I, has books and prior exams for sale as well; contact them at the address above. You may also want to consider enrolling your child in a prep course or hiring a private tutor for more personalized preparation.

THE ACT

The American College Test (ACT), administered by the American College Testing Company, is the other key college entrance exam. It's a three-hour, multiple-choice exam, and is very different from the PSAT and SAT I. The ACT is much more subject oriented than the SAT I. There are four sections on the ACT: English, Math, Reading, and Science Reasoning. The English test measures standard written English (punctuation, grammar and usage, and sentence structure) and rhetorical skills (strategy, organization and style); the Math test measures skills in arithmetic, algebra, geometry, and trigonometry; the Reading test measures reading comprehension; finally, the Science Reasoning test measures problem-solving skills in the natural sciences, including the physical sciences, biology, chemistry, and physics. Calculator use is not permitted on the ACT.

> "Don't assume that your kid's high school's SAT or ACT prep program will be right for him. Investigate private courses, software, and books."
>
> —High school senior,
> 1480 combined SAT score

ACT Scoring

ACT test takers receive four area test scores and one composite score, all scaled from 1 to 36. The average of the four area scores produce the composite score. The average area score is typically in the high teens or low 20s. The average composite ACT score has been near 21 in recent years. Seven subscores, ranging from 1 to 18, are also reported. Each subject area has subscores except the science reasoning section.

Taking the ACT

Students should take the ACT for the first time during the spring semester of their junior year; doing so allows them to study almost all of the material tested, and gives them the opportunity to retake the test if desired. Even more than with the SAT, taking a challenging curriculum throughout high school is the best way to prepare. In addition, there are books, software, and courses for ACT prep as well. For more information on the ACT contact: ACT Registration Department, P.O. Box 414, Iowa City, Iowa 52243-0414; phone (319) 337-1270.

SCHOOLS REQUIRING ONLY THE ACT
A SELECT LIST BY STATE

AL: Alabama A&M
Stillman

AK: Philander Smith

CA: Pacific Union

FL: U. of Southern Florida

HI: Brigham Young—
Hawaii

IA: Dordt

ID: Northwest Nazarene

IL: Northeastern Illinois
Olivet Nazarene
Southern Illinois—
Carbondale
U. of Illinois—Chicago

KS: Mid-America Nazarene
Pittsburg State

KY: Kentucky State
Lindsey Wilson
Murray State
Pikeville

LA: Louisiana State—
Shrevesport
Louisiana Tech
McNeese State
Northeast Louisiana
Our Lady of Holy
Cross
Southeastern Louisiana

MI: Andrews
Central Michigan
Ferris State
Oakland
St. Mary's
Wayne State
William Tyndale

MN: Bemidji State U.
Concordia College at
St. Paul
Metropolitan State
Moorehead State
St. Cloud State
U. of Minnesota at
Duluth and Morris
Winona State

MS: Jackson State
Rust

MO: Central Missouri State
Hannibal-LaGrange
Lincoln
Missouri Southern State
Missouri Western State
Northwest Missouri
State

ND: Jamestown

NE: Chadron State
College of St. Mary
Nebraska Wesleyan
Union

NM: New Mexico Institute
of Mining and
Technology
New Mexico State

OH: Mount Vernon
Nazarene
Shawnee State
U. of Findlay

OK: Cameron
East Central
Southern Nazarene
Southwestern
Oklahoma State
U. of Science and Arts

SD: Huron
South Dakota School
of Mines and
Technology
South Dakota State

TN: Crichton
Tennessee Tech.

TX: U. of Texas—Pan
American

UT: U. of Utah

WA: Walla Walla

WI: Alverno
Marian College of
Fond du Lac
U. of Wisconsin at
Green Bay, La Crosse,
Milwaukee, Oshkosh,
Platteville, Stevens
Point, Stout,
Superior, and Viterbo

THE PRELIMINARY ACT (P-ACT+)

The preliminary exam to the ACT is the Preliminary ACT or P-ACT+. The P-ACT+ is not considered to be a formal practice test for the ACT, but it does cover the same content and is presented in the same format. Since taking the P-ACT+ will help your child to become familiar with the ACT, he should take this exam during his sophomore year if it is offered at his school.

SCHOOLS REQUIRING ONLY THE SAT I

CA:	California Institute of Technology	MD:	Loyola		St. Thomas Aquinas
	Christian Heritage		Salisbury State	OR:	George Fox
	Harvey Mudd		Townson State	PA:	Allentown College of St. Francis deSales
	Santa Clara		U. of Maryland, Eastern Shore		
CT:	Central Connecticut State	ME:	St. Joseph's		Bloomsburg
	Eastern Connecticut State		U. of Maine— Orono and Presque Isle		Bryn Mawr
	St. Joseph				East Stroudsburg
	Southern Connecticut State	NC:	Fayetteville State		Haverford
	U. of Bridgeport		High Point		Lincoln
	Western Connecticut State		North Carolina State at Raleigh		Lock Haven
DC:	Catholic U of America	NH:	Keene State	RI:	Rhode Island College
GA:	Augusta	NJ:	Caldwell		Salve Regina
MA:	Bridgewater State		Georgian Court	TN:	Lane
	Mt. Holyoke		Keane	TX:	Ambassador
	Regis		Princeton		U. of Houston— Main Campus
	U. of Massachusetts— Dartmouth and Lowell		Ramapo	VA:	Hampton
			Rowan	VT:	Johnson State
	Westefield State		William Paterson		
		NY:	Dominican College of Blauvelt		
			Manhattanville		
			Marymount College, Tarrytown		
			St. Francis		

The ACT Versus the SAT

Should your child take the SAT I or ACT? Most colleges and universities in the United States accept both exams. Since the exams are different and high performance on one exam does not automatically translate into equally impressive performance on the other, be sure to determine which exam suits your child better and select that exam if her target schools accept it. The SAT I remains the more popular exam. The ACT, however, is gaining in popularity and is accepted by many colleges located in the southern, midwestern and western states. Some schools require only ACT scores for admission.

SCHOOL WITHOUT AN ACT OR SAT I REQUIREMENT: A SELECT LIST BY STATE (EXCLUDING SPECIALTY SCHOOLS)

AL: Sheldon Jackson

AZ: Prescott

CA: Golden Gate
Loma Linda
New College of California

DC: Garlander
U. of the District of Columbia

DE: Wilmington

GA: Brewton-Parkes
Thomas

HI: Hawaii Pacific

IL: Columbia
East-West

KS: Fort Hays State
Kansas State
Washburn State
Wichita State

MA: Endicott
Hampshire
Lasell
Mount Ida
Wheaton

MD: St. John's

ME: Bates
Bowdoin
College of the Atlantic
Unity
U. of Maine at Farmington

MI: Marygrove
Michigan Tech.
Olivet
U. of Michigan at Dearborn

MN: Crown

NE: Wayne State

NM: St. John's

NV: Sierra Nevada
U. of Nevada at Las Vegas

NY: Bard
Cazenovia
City University of New York (CUNY) at Brooklyn, City College, College of Staten Island, Hunter, Lehman, and York
Hilbert

Medaille

Mercy

State University of New York (SUNY) at Old Westbury, College of Arts and Sciences at Purchase, and Empire State U. of New York—Regents

OH: Antioch
Cleveland State
Tiffin
Union Institute

PA: Dickinson
Lafayette

RI: Johnson and Wales

SC: Benedict

TX: Texas Southern
Wiley

VT: Burlington
Goddard

WA: City University

Most of the ACT-only schools are located in the south and west. Many east coast schools require the SAT I only. And note that more than fifty schools do not require test scores from either exam.

Since the lists are not comprehensive, be sure your child contacts her target schools to determine whether they accept both the ACT and SAT I, or whether they require or prefer one test over the other. You can also consult college and university guidebooks to determine which exam is best for specific schools. These guidebooks will often also provide you with the percentage of students at the school submitting test scores for each exam. So, if a school says that it accepts both tests, but more than 90 percent of the students submitted the test scores for only one of the exams, your daughter would be better off taking that examination and submitting only those scores.

THE SAT II: SUBJECT TESTS

The SAT II: Subject Tests (formerly known as the Achievement Tests) are probably the most widely accepted content-based college entrance examinations used in the United States. They are administered by the Educational Testing Service (ETS) and

---

SAT II: SUBJECT TESTS

- **English**
  Literature
  Writing

- **Foreign Languages**
  Chinese (with listening)
  French (reading and with listening)
  German (reading and with listening)
  Italian (reading)
  Japanese with listening
  Latin (reading)
  Modern Hebrew (reading)
  Spanish (reading and with listening)

- **History and Social Studies**
  American History and Social Studies
  World History

- **Mathematics**
  Mathematics Level I (to geometry +)*
  Mathematics Level IIC (to trigonometry + and with calculator)*

- **Sciences**
  Biology
  Chemistry
  Physics

Note: Foreign language with listening exams are given at select high schools and are not given on the national test dates for the SAT I and SAT II exams. Contact your guidance office for more information for these test dates.

*Calculators for the SAT I and II tests should be capable of performing scientific functions (e.g., exponents).

---

are given on the same day as the SAT I (except for the foreign language exams with a listening component). On a given test date, you can take either the SAT I or up to three SAT IIs. Almost all SAT IIs are hour-long, multiple-choice examinations that measure your knowledge of that subject at the high school level. (The exception is the SAT II: Writing test, which is not completely multiple-choice—it includes an essay.) An ETS-produced booklet on the SAT IIs, available from the high school's guidance office, contains detailed descriptions of each exam with sample questions for each test. There are more than 20 tests that fall into five subject areas.

SAT II Scoring

The SAT II subject tests are scored on a scale of 200 to 800. These scores, like the SAT I scores, are reported to the colleges and universities that your child selects to receive score reports. Since the subject tests are being used by colleges for admissions purposes, these exams must be taken by December of senior year. Many competitive colleges request three or more subject test scores. Have your child consult her target schools to determine their admissions requirements. For more information on the SAT II subject tests, including examination dates and registration materials, write to: Admissions Testing Program, P.O. Box 6228, Princeton, NJ 08541-6228.

Taking SAT IIs

When should your child take the SAT II subject tests? She should take a test in a given area at the time she completes her studies in that area. This is when the material is fresh in her mind and she's most likely to achieve her highest score. If she completes chemistry at the end of her junior year, and she is applying to an engineering program and wants to demonstrate particular competence in the sciences, she should take her chemistry subject test in June of her junior year. In general, one year of solid high school preparation in a subject should be enough to score well on these exams. However, at least two years of foreign language study (of the same language) is recommended before taking an SAT II exam in that language.

Your child should take as many SAT IIs as he thinks that he will do well on. Many selective schools use SAT II scores to determine mastery of high school content, as well as for placement purposes and to determine whether a student can opt out of college graduation requirements (e.g., foreign language). Great scores on a variety of SAT IIs demonstrate mastery of subject areas at the high school level and are likely to impress an admissions committee. Students may also want to take SAT II exams in areas in which they have not done very well. For example, if your child received a 75 in chemistry, but believes that with some practice he could achieve a score of 600 or better on the SAT II, he should go ahead and take the exam. A good score on the SAT II in an area in which he has a low course grade could show that he knows more about a subject that the grade reflects. Like the SAT I, very competitive scores begin in the mid- to upper-600's.

ADVANCED PLACEMENT EXAMS (APs)

As described in detail in chapter one, the AP program allows students to pursue college-level work and earn college credit while still in high school. At the end of each course, you take a test that determines whether you've mastered the material well enough to earn college credit in that subject. For more information, see chapter one.

COLLEGE-LEVEL EXAMINATION PROGRAM (CLEP)

Sponsored by the College Board and administered by ETS, the College-Level Examination Program (CLEP) is another way to earn college credit by taking an exam. According to ETS, CLEP is the most widely accepted credit-by-examination program in the country, with more than 2,000 colleges and universities granting credit for satisfactory scores. CLEP test takers include high school students, adults returning to college, college students, and international students.

CLEP Subjects

There are 35 CLEP exams covering materials taught at the college level. These exams are 90 minutes long, and all but one are multiple-choice (the lone exception is the English exam with essay). The CLEP exams include:

- **General Examinations**
  English Composition (with or without essay)
  Humanities
  Mathematics
  Natural Sciences
  Social Sciences and History

- ## Subject-Specific Examinations
Composition and Literature:
American Literature
Analysis and Interpretation of Literature
College Composition
English Literature
Freshman English

Foreign Languages:
College French (Levels I—two semesters and II—four semesters)
College German (Levels I and II)
College Spanish (Levels I and II)

History and Social Sciences:
American Government
American History I: Early Colonization to 1877
American History II: 1865 to the Present
Human Growth and Development
Introduction to Educational Psychology
Introductory Macroeconomics
Introductory Microeconomics
Introductory Psychology
Introductory Sociology
Western Civilization I: Ancient Near East to 1648
Western Civilization II: 1648 to the Present

Science and Mathematics:
Calculus with Elementary Functions
College Algebra—Trigonometry
Trigonometry
General Biology
General Chemistry
Information Systems and Computer Applications
Introduction to Management
Introductory Accounting
Introductory Business Law
Principles of Marketing

The policy for granting credit based on CLEP scores varies by college. For information on the availability of CLEP and the granting of credits for CLEP, contact the admissions office at your target college or university; for a listing of colleges accepting CLEP, test centers and locations and other information, contact: CLEP, P.O. Box 6601, Princeton, NJ 08541-6601; phone (609) 951-1026.

SUMMARY

From winning scholarships and increasing chances of getting into a top school to achieving advanced placement in college courses, the rewards of doing well on standardized tests are many. So encourage your child to thoroughly prep for all the tests he'll take over his high school years.

For more tips on helping your teen prepare for standardized tests, visit Kaplan's Web site at www.kaplan.com/downloads/.

TELL YOUR TEEN

* Start preparing early for the admissions exams (no later than sophomore year).
* Take content-based exams right after you have completed the coursework.
* Attempt college-level courses and exams in at least two subject areas.

INTERNET RESOURCES

Testing Organizations

College Board Online. http://www.collegeboard.org
Register for the SAT I and order test-prep materials.

Educational Testing Service (ETS). http://www.ets.org/
For upcoming test dates and registration information for the
PSAT/NMSQT, SAT I, SAT II, and AP exams.

Test-Prep Services and Aids

Kaplan Educational Centers. http://www.kaplan.com/college
For test dates, sample tests, downloadable practice games, and test-taking strategies
for the PSAT, SAT I, and the ACT.

Syndicate. http://syndicate.com
Word puzzles, writing games, and other materials to help in vocabulary building
and essay writing.

CHAPTER 4

Extracurricular Activities

WHAT STUDENTS ASK

- **Why should I get involved in extracurricular activities?**
- **What are good activities to become involved in?**
- **How many activities is enough?**

Participating in extracurricular activities can help your child develop qualities like independence, enthusiasm, maturity, creativity, cooperation, leadership, commitment, self-motivation, and self-expression. She can boost her chances of getting into the college of her choice, since colleges seek people who will fuel and transform their communities through an active interest and participation in activities.

Your teen's goal throughout high school should be to actively participate in a range of diverse activities, and to excel in a few of them. While your child may pursue some activities just for fun, others may become consuming passions. But as rewarding as extracurricular activities can be, it's important that your son or daughter keeps academic excellence at the forefront of all of his or her plans. The coursework represents the foundation on which your child's extracurricular involvement should be built.

HOW INVOLVED SHOULD HE GET?

Your child's level of involvement can run the gamut from dabbling (occasionally attending meetings) to leadership (presiding over a group). He may want to

"High school students need to explore their limits. Find out what your kids are interested in and encourage them. Make the opportunities available and make them attractive."

—High school senior

become an active member who will accept more responsibility for setting the direction of the group, or participate as a general member where attendance is key. Her level of involvement will vary based on her level of interest in each activity and the amount of time she has to devote. Your child should pick at least one (preferably two) activities that she will progress in during her high school years. Establishing concrete goals is the first step to achieving them.

WHAT TO CHOOSE?

The possibilities are nearly limitless: Your child can get involved in activities in his high school, in your community, or somewhere else in the United States or overseas. Choosing the right activity for him can be overwhelming, but the first place he should start is thinking about which skills or interests he would most like to pursue. After he has figured this out, the next step is developing an activity plan that will meet his needs. Basically, he can choose to pursue interests on his own, after school, or in the summer.

INDEPENDENT STUDY

Some students find that they learn well on their own and enjoy the ability to proceed at their own pace. Does this describe your child? If so, she may want to pursue her interest independently, on her own terms. Independent study is probably the most difficult way of pursuing activities while in high school. It requires discipline, self-motivation, and an ability to teach yourself complex materials.

To begin an independent-study project, a student must define the scope of the activity (e.g., to learn a foreign language or a musical instrument), establish objectives (e.g., to gain fluency in reading, writing, and speaking, or to be able to follow and play from complex sheet music), determine what materials he needs to meet his objectives (e.g., books, tapes, and lessons), and schedule work to meet these objectives (e.g., practice). Sound tough? It is—studying on your own requires tremendous discipline. But the rewards are great: Your child can pursue his interests at an advanced level while sharpening basic academic skills like reading, vocabulary, and writing. He'll also enjoy the freedom of controlling his own pace, choosing which interests to pursue, and starting a new study program whenever he chooses to begin it.

There are many self-study activities that your child can pursue in her spare time. Here's one example of how she can improve basic reading skills as an independent learner.

SELF-STUDY PROJECT—INDEPENDENT READING

Project: Independent reading

Objectives:
- To become well read
- To strengthen reading comprehension and vocabulary skills before taking the SAT I
- To build a résumé of reading experience for college applications and interviews
- To easily answer the following questions:
    - What books have you read in the past year?
    - Why were these books chosen?
    - Did the books meet your expectations? Why?
    - What have you learned from them?
    - What topics or authors did you like most? Least? Why?
    - What would you like to read in the future?

Even though she'll be studying on her own, she might want to hook up with some sort of support network to bolster her efforts. You can find some of these in the Internet Resources section of chapter one.

AFTER-SCHOOL PROGRAMS

After-school programs offer an excellent opportunity for students to pursue their interests. Subjects range from academics, to the arts, to cultural activities and community affairs. You may find that your child's school already has an existing club or organization that interests him. Or, he may choose to form an organization himself or with friends.

Here are some subjects for after-school activities and programs. We've provided an overview of each general area, included a sample list of activities for each, and shown an example of possible clubs or activities you can organize or join.

English

If your child is interested in English in school, she can pursue her interest after hours in a variety of ways: having fun with language fundamentals, teaching others, creative writing, or building communication skills.

Related Clubs

Comedy Magazine
Debate Team
Drama Club
English Club
Film Society
Journalism Club
Literary Magazine
Mock Trial Team
Newspaper
Poets Society
Political Journal
Radio Station
Science Fiction Club
Shakespeare Club
Tutoring (remedial English or ESL)
Video- and Filmmaking Club
Yearbook

Suggest These Possible Activities

- You could get involved in a literacy project, and help young people or adults learn to read. Students would spend an hour or two each week with their partner, working on his or her reading skills.
- A study group could read and discuss the works of William Shakespeare. Members could also attend local movies, plays and lectures featuring Shakespeare's works. They could then meet and discuss these works in detail.
- You could start an open mic performance group, where students could read their poems, stories, monologues, or plays. Readings could be open to the community, or kept for students only.
- A film club could attend and discuss films released by independent filmmakers and major studios.

Social Studies

Social studies includes those topics that involve people and their societies the world over. This includes the study and expression of culture, language, lifestyles, religion, government, community affairs. If your child is interested in current events and different cultures, here are some possible activities for him:

"Being organized is key. I stayed after school until 5:00 for my activities, then came home and did my homework right away, without fail."

—Freshman, Drew University

Related Clubs
AIDS Education and Outreach Committee
African American Students Association
Asian American Students Association
Big Brother/Big Sister programs
Catholic Students Association
Christian Fellowship
Democrat Club
Environmental Action League
Hellenic Cultural Society
Homelessness Action Committee
Irish Cultural and Historical Society
International Students Association
Language table or club
Model U.N.
Republican Club
Scouts (Boys or Girls)
Student Government
Students Against Drunk Driving
Third World Student Alliance

Suggest These Possible Activities
- Hillel (Jewish Students Association) activities could include a Hebrew language table, Bible or Talmudic study and discussion groups, and trips to events and local institutions celebrating Jewish history and culture.
- If you're concerned about the environment, you could help clean up a local wildlife area, get involved with a nearby Sierra Club branch, or organize other students to lobby for particular issues.

Mathematics and the Sciences

If your child enjoys studying math or science, he could get involved in a group that is academic (like a biology study group) or geared toward applied study (like a Future Physicians group). Here are some examples:

Related Clubs

Anthropology Club
Biology Newsletter
Computer Society
Future Physicians Society
Junior Academy of Science
Math Team
Science Club
Space Research Society

Suggest These Possible Activities

- The Computer Society members might get together to create a program that would be helpful to the school; talk about new software or Web sites; help students or faculty learn new software; or play games.
- The Future Physicians Society could organize speakers to discuss health issues in the community; coordinate volunteer efforts at a local hospital; or discuss changes in health care.

Foreign Languages

Often the study of a foreign language is combined with a study of a country or region where the language is spoken, so look in the social studies section for ideas on pursuing cultural activities. Students in language clubs often meet to practice speaking their language, or go to cultural events where their particular language is spoken.

Business Education

The goal of many business-based activities is to gain exposure to the world of work and to establish contact with local leaders. Activities can include the following:

Related Clubs

Business Club
Junior Achievement

Suggest These Possible Activities

- Business club members could organize a career fair featuring local businesses and workshops on preparing a résumé, building interviewing skills, and finding part-time and summer jobs.

Fine/Performing Arts

Fine and performing arts groups can include clubs that provide an opportunity for individual expression, as well as those that organize students to attend performances, museums, and other exhibits.

Related Clubs

Art Society
Architecture and Design Society
Color Guard
Cheerleading Squad
Choral Society
Dance Group
Glee Club
Jazz Band
Marching Band
Orchestra
Photography Club
Theater Club
Wind Ensemble

Suggest These Possible Activities

- The Theater Club might perform a musical comedy; members could perform in the cast, design and create sets, choreograph dance routines, and publicize the event in the community.

There are hundreds of potential activities for students to become involved in during high school. These activities provide an excellent way for them to learn and demonstrate skills and personal qualities that admissions officers value while also developing interests and friendships that are valuable for years to come.

POSTGRADUATION PROGRAMS

Students can choose to pursue many of the activities listed above during summer vacations. But your child could also choose to defer college for a year and immerse himself in some other activity. Each year thousands of students take time off between high school and college to work, study, or travel. Their reasons are often good enough for a college or university to grant a deferral (i.e., hold a place for a student at their school). The typical deferment period is one year (only in exceptional circumstances will the more selective schools hold a place for you for more than a year).

If your child plans to defer admission for a year after graduating high school, she still should complete the college application and selection process while in high school. It's easier to take standardized tests when you have just finished the materials, and to get letters of recommendation from school administrators, teachers, and employers while they can still remember your name and contributions.

> **TIME OFF**
>
> Each year thousands of students take a year off between high school and college to work, study, or travel. If your teen is considering deferring college for a year, have her contact her target schools and ask about their deferment policy.

SUMMER CAMPS

Almost all students find that they have time on their hands during the summer months. This is often the best time to learn a new skill, donate time to a public service activity, or develop a new interest. One way of doing this is by attending summer camp. Camps range from the wholly recreational to those providing advanced instruction in special subject areas. Listed below some sampling of organized ways to spend summers.

Academic Enrichment
Academic Study Associates
355 Main Street, Box 800
Armonk, NY 10504
(800) 752-2250

Computer—ED
P.O. Box 177
Weston, MA 02193
(800) 341-4433

Adventure
Biosearch College
High School Afloat Program
(800) 915-2655

Architecture
Summer Academy for Architecture
Roger Williams University School of Architecture
One Ferry Road
Bristol, RI 02809
(401) 254-3605

Dramatic Arts
American Academy of Dramatic Arts
2550 Paloma Street
Pasadena, CA 91107
(Also has a New York–based program; call: (212) 686-9244 for more information
on courses at both locations.)

Stagedoor Manor
Performing Arts Training Center
130 Wood Hollow Lane
New Rochelle, NY 10804
(914) 636-8578

Language
Rassias Foundation at Dartmouth College
6071-T Wentworth Hall
Hanover, NH 03755-3526
(603) 646-2922

Leadership
Junior Statesmen Summer Schools
Held at the U. of Texas at Austin, Standford, Yale, Georgetown, and Northwestern
Call (800) 334-5353 for more information.

The Next Generation Leadership Program
George Washington U. Summer Sessions
2121 I Street, NW 602F
Washington, DC 20052
(202) 994-6360

Math

Summermath
Mount Holyoke College
South Hadley, MA 01075
(413) 538-2608
(A program for girls.)

Music

Luzerne Music Center
P.O. Box 35
Lake Luzerne, NY 12846
(800) 874-3202

New England Music Camp
549 Spring Street
Manchester, CT 06040
(860) 646-1642

Science

Acadia Institute of Oceanography
Box 89
Kittery, ME 03904
(207) 439-2733

U. S. Space Camp and Space Academy
One Tranquility Base
Huntsville, AL 35807
(800) 63-SPACE

Service

American Jewish Society for Service
15 E. 26th Street, Room 1029
New York, NY 10010
(212) 683-6178

Studio Arts

Accelerated Program in Art
Office of the Dean of Special Programs

Skidmore College
815 North Broadway
Saratoga Springs, NY 12866-1632
(518) 584-5000, ext. 2264

Summer Programs/CE
Rhode Island School of Design
2 College Street
Providence, RI 02903-2787
(800) 262-4237

For more information on finding a general, specialty, academic, or travel summer camp, contact: The National Camp Association, 610 Fifth Avenue, New York, NY 10185; phone (800) 262-4237. Request a copy of their pamphlet, How to Choose a Summer Camp. You can also call the American Camping Association (ACA) for listings of ACA-qualified camps: (800) 428-2267 or (212) 268-7822 (in New York City). Finally, at the end of this chapter, there is a listing of camp and summer program sites on the Internet. You can consult these areas for more specific information on programs in your geographic and/or subject areas of interest. When contacting any of these organizations, ask for a program description, schedule, information on fees, and the availability of financial aid.

STUDY ABROAD

While summer camps provide an opportunity to learn new skills and interact with motivated students in the United States, there are other programs that provide similar experiences on a more global level. Students can learn about other countries and cultures first-hand through summer travel and study-abroad programs.

In general, three types of travel programs are available to high school students:

Travel. Sight-seeing with visits to the country's top attractions.

Study. Formal study of language or culture, with travel.

Volunteer. Combines travel with community service: work in a group on a neighborhood clean-up, kibbutz, or other community project.

These programs vary significantly by country, what is offered, degree of supervision, availability of school credit, and so on. If your child is interested in traveling abroad during summer vacation or spending a year during or after high school traveling and studying, investigate these programs.

When you or your child contacts travel and study abroad programs, be sure to get the following information:

- Sponsoring organization: Who is the program coordinator?
- Location: Which countries are involved?
- Activities involved: Are these travel, study, service or "other" programs?
- Length of stay: What is the program's length?
- Requirements: Is there an age requirement? Language or academic prerequisites?
- Cost: Is financial aid available?
- Living arrangements: Where do students live? Are there "host" families?
- Academic credit: Does the program offer it? Does your school accept it?
- Degree of supervision: Who's in charge of you while you are away?

Finding a good sponsoring organization is key to finding a good program. The number of organizations offering high school programs abroad have grown rapidly in the last ten years. Buyer beware: A good brochure does not necessarily equal a good program. Find out if the sponsoring organization is a for-profit corporation or nonprofit organization dedicated to international exchange. Ask the sponsoring organization for the names of past participants (or their parents) that you can talk to. Get advice from high school guidance counselors. And read the brochure, including the fine print, carefully. Make sure you get direct answers to all of your questions.

Finding a Program Abroad

A good place to start is the directory published by the nonprofit Council on Standards for International Educational Travel (CSIET). This organization investigates organizations offering educational programs abroad for high school students and includes in its directory only those programs that have met its standards. The directory, *The Advisory List of International Educational Travel and Exchange Programs*, is published annually and available for $10 from CSIET. Your child's high school guidance office may have a copy. CSIET will also answer questions about the organizations it has listed over the phone; call to find out if a particular organization has met its standards. You can contact CSIET at 3 Loudoun Street SE, Leesburgh, VA 221175; telephone (703) 771-2040.

Whether you are looking for a program for a year, a semester, a summer, or only during spring break, you will probably want to contact these three nonprofit organizations: AFS (formerly known as American Field Service), World Learning (formerly known as the Experiment in International Living), and Youth for Understanding (YFU). These three organizations have led the way in developing and running programs all over the world for high school students. Most of their programs offer various combinations of travel, study, sports, and/or living with a host family abroad.

AFS Intercultural Programs
220 East 42nd Street, 3rd Floor
New York, NY 10017
(800) AFS-INFO

YFU
U.S. National Office
3501 Newark Street NW
Washington, DC 20016
(800) TEENAGE

World Learning
Summer Abroad Programs
P.O. Box SAPG
Brattleboro, VT 05302
(800) 345-2929

In addition to the above, two other major organizations offering a range of high school programs abroad are:

ASSE International Student Exchange Programs
228 North Coast Highway
Laguna Beach, CA 92651
(714) 494-4100

EF Education Foundation for Foreign Study
204 Lake Street
Boston, MA 02135
(800) 992-1892

If your child just wants travel without even the pretense of study, there are a number of options for group tours for high school students. Two organizations that pioneered group tours abroad for high school students are the nonprofit Hostelling International/American Youth Hostels (HI/AYH) and the for-profit company Putney Student Travel. They continue to offer a variety of types of high school group tours to all corners of the world. In recent years many other for-profit companies have sprung up to enter this growing market—too many to begin to list all of them here. Check for advertisements in the travel section of the Sunday edition of any large metropolitan newspaper.

American Youth Hostels Discovery Tours
HI-AYH National Office
7331 15th Street NW, #840
Washington, SC 20005
(202) 783-6161

Putney Student Travel
345 Hickory Ridge Road
Putney, VT 05346
(802) 387-5885

If your child wants to travel independently, either alone or with a group of friends, but not on a preorganized group tour, there are two travel organizations, STA and Council Travel, you should know about. Both focus on student travel and provide student discounts, including discounts on international airlines, that are not available to the general public. In addition to offering travel services via an 800 number, both organizations also have walk-in offices across the country, most of which are near large university campuses. You can contact Council Travel at (800) 2-COUNCIL, or check their Web site at http://www.ciee.org. You can call STA at (800) 777-0112, or via the Internet at http://www.sta~travel.com.

Yet another option is the school-to-school exchange, which involves a partnership between your child's school and a school abroad. This type of program is usually the cheapest option for overseas travel. It involves 2–4 weeks of traveling and attending school abroad. A group of student from your school visit a school, travel, attend classes, and stay in the homes of other students. Then a reciprocal visit occurs in which your school hosts students from the partner school abroad. You can't participate in a program of this type as an individual unless your school is linked up, but you can check to see if your school has such a program or is interested in starting one. Two nonprofit organizations that will set your school up with a partner school abroad and arrange the trip are the Council on International Educational Exchange (CIEE) and the National Association of Secondary School Principals (NASSP).

School Partners Abroad
Council on International Educational Exchange
205 East 42nd Street
New York, NY 10017
(800) 2-COUNCIL

Parnerships International
National Association of Secondary School Principals
1904 Association Drive
Reston, VA 22091
(800) 253-7746

One good source of further information is the magazine *Transitions Abroad*, which contains a large number of articles and advertisements on study, work, volunteer, and travel opportunities abroad. For a subscription ($24.95 per year for six issues), write Transitions Abroad, Dept. TRA, Box 3000, Denville, NJ 07843. For an excellent source of general advice—although the specific information is now somewhat out of date—check in a library or bookstore for the book, *The High School Student's Guide to Study, Travel, and Adventure Abroad*, written by the Council on International Educational Exchange and published by St. Martin's Press in 1993.

For additional companies sponsoring foreign-exchange and travel-abroad programs with sites on the Internet, consult the listings at the end of this chapter.

SPORTS

Your teenager may play a sport just for fun, or she may be determined to pursue her sport seriously and play in college, or even professionally. Whatever the case, participating in sports can be a way to get fit, make friends, and learn discipline and goal setting.

There are generally five levels of involvement in high school sports: recreational, intramural, junior varsity, varsity, and professional. What makes each level different is the skill of the athletes involved, and the amount of structure surrounding recruitment, player selection, practice, and competitive play. The emphasis on each of these elements is greater as you move up the hierarchy of play.

Recreational Activity

Playing at the recreational level is great for students looking for an introduction to a sport, sheer fun, or the opportunity to practice and hone their skills. Recreational activity includes everything from informal outings to local pick-up games and matches. In these informal activities there may be very skilled players involved, but you don't need to be skilled to participate.

Intramural

The level of organization, like the skill required to compete at this level, ranges from minimal to extensive. Intramural play includes competitive events sponsored by members within the same school, extracurricular group, or community (e.g., ninth grade versus tenth grade students or a community-sponsored track-and-field event). Typically, players at this level are familiar with the rules of the game and have had some prior exposure to the sport.

Junior Varsity

At the JV level, students get uniforms to play in and can become eligible for a JV letter. Only students with previous experience in the sport are likely to participate in JV, since you generally need to try out to qualify for the team. If the JV team is then used to recruit, train, monitor, and select athletes for the varsity level, the skill required and the structure surrounding play is likely to be moderate to high.

Varsity

At the varsity level, competition is usually governed by a local or regional body. Varsity play is often the highest level of competition available for high school athletes. From this level, a few exceptional students and teams are able to compete in statewide, national, and international events. Many great varsity players are scouted and recruited by colleges and the occasional professional team.

"My schoolwork always comes first. I'm editor of the school newspaper, in the band, involved in wrestling. Being involved in all these activities helps keep me organized."

—High school senior

Professional

Still fewer student athletes are able to attain professional status. At this level, competition is governed by national and international bodies (such as United States Tennis Association and the International Tennis Federation) and individual athletes must demonstrate superior skill in order to compete successfully against equally skilled professionals in the sport.

ATHLETIC SCHOLARSHIPS

If your teen is a top performer in a sport and a college happens to need players like him, she may get a partial or full athletic scholarship to college. Most private colleges award scholarships on a case-by-case basis, but some colleges don't give out athletic scholarships at all. Even if athletic scholarships are not available at the colleges of your child's choice, she may want to contact the coaching staff at her target schools to make them aware of her talent and interest in competing on their team.

NATIONAL COLLEGIATE ATHLETIC ASSOCIATION (NCAA)

If your son is interested in pursuing your sport at the highest level of amateur competition available while in college, contact the National Collegiate Athletic Association (NCAA) and its member schools. Founded in 1906, the NCAA is the oldest and best known collegiate sports organization in the country. The NCAA is the governing body for athletic competition at over 900 colleges across the United States. Each year, more than 20,000 students compete on NCAA teams in more than 20 sports.

Eligibility

The NCAA determines academic eligibility requirements for the sports programs of its member schools. Students hoping to play on teams at NCAA schools must meet specific criteria, including minimum SAT I and ACT scores, in order to be eligible for athletic scholarships and competitive play.

Eligibility requirements and availability of athletic scholarships at NCAA schools depends on the level that the college participates in NCAA activities. The NCAA maintains three separate divisions with specific rules for each. The Division I schools, of which there are more than 300, represent the country's major college athletic programs. Division I athletic programs often benefit from revenue generated from the broadcast of football and basketball games sanctioned by the NCAA. The nearly 250 Division II schools also have a number of competitive athletic programs, but their programs and the extent of the scholarships offered are smaller than that of Division I schools. Division III schools, of which there are more than 350, don't provide scholarships, but do offer extensive athletic programs.

NCAA Division I

Division I and II schools are able to award scholarships based on athletic ability. Their applicants, however, are subject to academic eligibility requirements. According to new rules adopted in the summer of 1996, the criteria include graduating from high school with a minimum GPA in at least 13 core college prep courses (each course is equal to one year of study at the high school level), like those outlined in the first chapter, with a sliding scale for standardized test scores to enable a high test score to offset a low GPA.

NCAA DIVISION I ELIGIBILITY CURRICULUM	
Subject	**Requirements**
English	4 years
Math	2 years (algebra and geometry)
Science	2 years (with 1 year of laboratory science)
Social Studies	2 years
+ English, math, or science	1 year
+ English, math, science, foreign language, computer science, philosophy, or religion	2 years

A student qualifies with a minimum GPA of 2.5 and a SAT I test score of 820 or a combined ACT score of 68. According to the sliding scale, a student with a higher GPA of 2.75 but lower test scores of 720 on the SAT I or a combined ACT score of 59 would also be eligible to receive a first-year scholarship. A student with a lower GPA of 2.0, however, would need higher test scores of 1010 or 86 on the SAT I or

ACT, respectively, to be eligible to play on an NCAA Division I team as a college freshman.

If you're not sure whether your child meets the NCAA's eligibility requirements, have him check with his coach or contact the NCAA for the latest information on eligibility rules and guidelines.

NCAA Division II

To be eligible to play on a Division II team, students must also meet NCAA eligibility requirements. They include graduating from high school and having a GPA of 2.0 in thirteen courses.

To qualify, students must also score am 820 or above on the SAT I or receive a minimum combined score of 68 on the ACT.

NCAA DIVISION II ELIGIBILITY CURRICULUM	
Subject	**Requirements**
English	3 years
Math	2 years
Science	2 years (including 1 year of a lab science)
Social Studies	2 years
+ English, math, or science	1 year
+ Above categories or a foreign language, computer science, philosophy, or religion	2 years

NCAA Division III

NCAA Division III schools do not award scholarships based on athletic ability; they can only provide financial aid based on demonstrated financial need. Division III applicants, however, are not subject to the NCAA's academic eligibility criteria. Have your daughter check with her coach or consult with her target schools and ask about their NCAA Division standing for your sport and the current NCAA eligibility requirements for athletic scholarships and play in their programs.

You can get more information on NCAA athletic programs and scholarships from the following NCAA publications: *NCAA Guide for the College Bound Student-Athlete,* the *NCAA Manual,* and the *NCAA Clearinghouse Brochure and Form.* Or write for a free copy to: The NCAA, 6201 College Boulevard, Overland Park, KS 66211-2422; phone (913) 339-1906. Or call the NCAA Hotline at (800) 638-3731. The Hotline features a recorded message covering freshman eligibility, the NCAA Clearinghouse, recruiting rules and information, and information and rules on transferring from two-year colleges to four-year schools.

If your child is planning to qualify for a NCAA Division I or II team, be sure that she is registered with the NCAA Initial-Eligibility Clearinghouse no later than the spring of her junior year of high school, or she won't be able to play on a Division I or II team during her freshman year. You can contact the Clearinghouse at: NCAA Clearinghouse, P.O. Box 4043, Iowa City, IA 52243-4043; phone (319) 339-3003, (319) 337-1492, or fax (319) 337-1556 for more information and to receive a copy of the brochure *Making Sure You Are Eligible to Participate in College Sports.*

NATIONAL JUNIOR COLLEGE ATHLETIC ASSOCIATION (NJCAA) AND THE NATIONAL ASSOCIATION OF INTERCOLLEGIATE ATHLETICS (NAIA)

There are two other major governing bodies of intercollegiate activity: The National Junior College Athletic Association (NJCAA), and the National Association of Intercollegiate Athletics (NAIA). The NJCAA is the body most responsible for coordinating intercollegiate competition among major two-year colleges in the United States. The NAIA is present at about 400 smaller four-year colleges and universities. The member schools of the NJCAA do not recruit as heavily as NCAA schools, but they do recruit students and are allowed to pay for student visits to their campuses. NAIA member schools also don't recruit heavily, and they are not allowed to pay for student-athlete visits to their campuses. To find out more information about the NJCAA and NAIA, their member schools and regulations governing recruitment and eligibility to play, contact: National Junior College Athletic Association, P.O. Box 7305, Colorado Springs, CO 80933-7305; phone (719) 590-9788, and/or the National Association of Intercollegiate Athletics, 6120 South Yale Avenue, Suite 1450, Tulsa, Oklahoma 74136-4223; phone (918) 494-8828.

NATIONAL CHRISTIAN COLLEGE ATHLETIC ASSOCIATION (NCCAA)

If your child is considering attending a Christian college and is planning to be active in their athletic programs, write to: National Christian College Athletic Association (NCCAA), P.O. Box 1312, Marion, IN 46952; phone (317) 674-8401 for their directory of member schools.

CONTACTING COACHES

If your teen is interested in playing a sport at any level in college, he should consider contacting coaches in his target schools before he applies. Encourage him to send a letter describing his current level of participation in the sport, and ask for the following information about the school's athletic program:

- Conference participation and eligibility requirements
- Description of the training and on-campus playing facilities
- Team history (including last year's performance)
- Information about the coach and returning players
- Length and schedule of the playing season

Students should begin to identify and write to college coaches no later than the fall of junior year. This will give interested coaches enough time to follow their progress before they begin applying to their school during the senior year.

OTHER ATHLETIC ORGANIZATIONS

Numerous organizations coordinate competition and send out useful information about opportunities in specific sports. This information includes newsletters, schedules of local sporting events, and scholarships. To find out about opportunities in his sport of interest, your teen can contact the appropriate organizations listed below or ask his high school coach for more information.

National Organizations

National Archery Association
One Olympic Plaza
Colorado Springs, CO 80909
(719) 578-4576

U.S. Badminton Association
One Olympic Plaza
Colorado Springs, CO 80909
(719) 578-4808

U.S.A. Baseball
2160 Greenwood Avenue
Trenton, NJ 08609
(609) 586-2381

U.S.A. Basketball
5465 Mark Dabling Boulevard
Colorado Springs, CO 80918-3842
(719) 590-4800

U.S. Biathlon Association
P.O. Box 5515
Essex Junction, VT 05453
(802) 655-4524

U.S. Bobsled and Skeleton Federation
P.O. Box 828 (421 Old Military Road)
Lake Placid, NY 12948
(518) 523-1842

Young American Bowling Alliance
5301 South 76 Street
Greendale, WI 53129-1194
(414) 421-4700

U.S.A. Boxing
One Olympic Plaza
Colorado Springs, CO 80909
(719) 578-4506

American Canoe Association
7432 Alban Station Boulevard
Suite B-226
Springfield, VA 22150
(703) 451-0141

U.S. Cycling Federation
One Olympic Plaza
Colorado Springs, CO 80909
(719) 578-4581

U.S. Diving, Inc.
Pan American Plaza, Suite 430
201 South Capitol Avenue
Indianapolis, IN 46225
(317) 237-5252

U.S. Fencing Association
One Olympic Plaza
Colorado Springs, CO 80909-5774
(719) 578-4511

U.S.A. Field Hockey Association
1750 East Boulder Street
Colorado Springs, CO 80909-5773
(719) 578-4567

U.S. Figure Skating Association
20 First Street
Colorado Springs, CO 80906-3697
(719) 635-5200

All-American Collegiate Golf Foundation
555 Madison Avenue
New York, NY 10022
(212) 751-5170

U.S.A. Gymnastics
Pan American Plaza, Suite 300
201 South Capitol Avenue
Indianapolis, IN 46225
(317) 237-5050

Amateur Hockey Association
of the U.S.
4965 North 30th Street
Colorado Springs, CO 80919
(719) 599-5500

American Horse Shows Association
220 East 42 Street, Suite 409
New York, NY 10017-5876
(212) 972-2472

Intercollegiate Horse Shows
Association
Smoke Run Farm
Hollow Road, Box 741
Stony Brook, NY 11790
(516) 751-2803

United States Judo, Inc.
P.O. Box 10013
El Paso, TX 79991
(915) 565-8754

U.S. Luge Association
P.O. Box 651 (35 Church Street)
Lake Placid, NY 12946
(518) 523-2071

U.S. Modern Pentathlon Association
530 McCullough
San Antonio, TX 78215
(210) 246-3000

American Amateur Racquetball
Association
1685 West Ulntah
Colorado Springs, CO 80904
(719) 635-5396

U.S. Amateur Confederation of
Roller Skating
P.O. Box 6579 (4730 South Street)
Lincoln, NE 68506
(402) 483-7551

U.S. Rowing Association
201 South Capitol Avenue, Suite 400
Indianapolis, IN 46225
(317) 237-5656

U.S. Sailing Association
P.O. Box 209
Newport, RI 02840
(401) 683-0800

U.S.A. Shooting
One Olympic Plaza
Colorado Springs, CO 80909
(719) 578-4670

U.S. Skiing
P.O. Box 100 (1500 Kearns Boulevard)
Park City, UT 84060
(801) 649-9090

U.S. Squash Racquet Association
P.O. Box 1216 (23 Cynwyd Road)
Bala Cynwyd, PA 19004
(610) 667-4006

U.S. Soccer Federation
1801-1811 South Prairie Avenue
Chicago, IL 60616
(312) 808-1300

Amateur Softball Association
2801 N. E. 50th Street
Oklahoma City, OK 78111-7203
(405) 424-5266

U.S. Swimming, Inc.
One Olympic Plaza
Colorado Springs, CO 80909
(719) 578-4578

U.S. Synchronized Swimming, Inc.
Pan American Plaza, Suite 910
201 South Capitol Avenue
Indianapolis, IN 46225
(317) 237-5700

U.S.A. Table Tennis
One Olympic Plaza
Colorado Springs, CO 80909
(719) 578-4583

U.S. Tae Kwon Do Union
One Olympic Plaza, Suite 405
Colorado Springs, CO 80909
(719) 578-4632

U.S. Team Handball Federation
One Olympic Plaza
Colorado Springs, CO 80909-5768
(719) 578-4582

U.S. Tennis Association
70 West Red Oak Lane
White Plains, NY 10604
(914) 696-7000

U.S.A. Track and Field
P.O. Box 120 (1 Hoosier Dome,
Suite 140)
Indianapolis, IN 46206
(317) 261-0500

Triathlon Federation U.S.A.
3595 East Fountain Boulevard, Suite F-1
Colorado Springs, CO 80910
(719) 597-9090

U.S. Volleyball Association
3595 East Fountain Boulevard, Suite I-2
Colorado Springs, CO 80910-1740
(719) 637-8300

U.S. Water Polo
1685 West Uintah
Colorado Spring, CO 80904-2921
(719) 634-0699

American Water Ski Association
799 Overlook Drive, SE
Winter Haven, FL 33884
(941) 324-4341

U.S. Weightlifting Federation
One Olympic Plaza
Colorado Springs, CO 80909-5764
(719) 578-4508

U.S.A. Wrestling
6155 Lehman Drive
Colorado Springs, CO 80918
(719) 598-8181

Intercollegiate Yacht Racing Association
 of North America
8893 Melinda Court
Milan, MI 48160

Community Organizations

Amateur Athletic Union
c/o Walt Disney World Resort
P.O. Box 10000
Lake Buena Vista, FL 32830
(407) 363-6170

Boys and Girls Clubs of America
1230 West Peachtree Street, NW
Atlanta, GA 30309
(404) 815-5700

Catholic Youth Organization
1011 First Avenue
New York, NY 10022
(212) 371-1000

National Exploring Division
Boy Scouts of America
1325 West Walnut Hill Lane
P.O. Box 152079 (8210)
Irving, TX 75015
(972) 580-2423

National Association of Police Athletic
 Leagues
618 U.S. Highway 1 , Suite 201
North Palm Beach, FL 33408
(561) 844-1823

National Congress of State Games
P.O. Box 2318
Billings, MT 59103
(406) 255-7426

Women's Sports

National Association for Girls and
 Women in Sports
1900 Association Drive
Reston, VA 22091
(703) 476-3450

Women's Sports Foundation
Eisenhower Park
East Meadow, NY 11554
(516) 542-4700

Athletes with Disabilities

American Athletic Association of the
 Deaf, Inc.
3607 Washington Boulevard, #4
Ogden, UT 84403-1737
tel. (801) 393-8710
fax (801) 393-2263

U.S. Cerebral Palsy Athletic Association
500 South Ervay, Suite 452B
Dallas, TX 75201
(214) 761-0033

National Handicapped Sports
451 Huugerford Drive, Suite 100
Rockville, MD 20850
(301) 217-0960

Wheelchair Sports U.S.A.
3595 East Fountain Boulevard, Suite L-1
Colorado Springs, CO 80910
(719) 574-1150

U.S. Association for Blind Athletes
33 North Institute
Colorado Springs, CO 80903
(719) 630-0422

Sports Camps

Basketball
Menominee Basketball Camp
4985 Highway D
Eagle River, WI 54521
(800) 236-CAMP)

Pro Shot Basketball Camp
142 River Road
Thornhurst, PA 18424
(717) 842-7044

St. Mary's College Seahawk
Basketball Camp
St. Mary's College
St. Mary's City, MD 20686
(301) 862-0310

Football
A.S.C. Contact Football and Kicking
Camps at St. Edward's U
A.S.C. Football Camps, Inc.
(800) 272-7017

Offense-Defense and Kicking Football
 Camps (California)
P.O. Box 9391
Glendale, CA 91226

Offense-Defense Football Camps
 (New York)
SUNY at Stony Brook
Stony Brook, NY 11794
(800) 243-4296

Golf
Golf Camp
Brewster Academy
Wolfeboro, NH 03894
(610) 642-1933

JKST Golf School Summer Camp
JKST, Inc.
Haverford College
Haverford. PA 19041
(610) 243-0678

Silver Sands Golf Academy
563 Upper Gardens Road
Fontana, WI 53125
(414) 275-6122

Gymnastics
Spotlight Gymnastics International
901 Pelhamdale Avenue
Pelham Manor, NY 10803
(914) 699-8335

Ice Hockey and Figure Skating
Elite Hockey Camp at Brooks School
c/o Brooks School
North Andover, MA 01845
(508) 686-6101

Figure Skating Camp at Lake Placid
National Sports Academy at Lake Placid
12 Lake Placid Club Drive
Lake Placid, NY 12946
(518) 523-3460

Martial Arts
Otis Ridge Camp for the Martial Arts
P.O. Box 20
Otis, MA 02153
(800) 528-0880

Riding
International Riding Camp
Birdhall Road
Greenfield Park, NY 12435
(914) 647-3240

Road's End Farm Horsemanship Center
T. T. Woodman
Chesterfield, NH 03443
(603) 363-4900

Sprucelands Equestrian Center
and Summer Camp
Pit Road
P.O. Box 54
Java Center, NY 10482
(716) 457-4150

Rowing
Craftsbury Sculling Camp
The Craftsbury Sports Center
Box 31
Craftsbury Common, VT 05827
(800) 729-7751

Sailing
Action Sail—Actionquest
P.O. Box 5507
Sarasota, FL 34277
(941) 924-6789

Sail Caribbean
79 Church Street
Northport, NY 11768
(800) 321-0994

Soccer
Connecticut Soccer School
c/o Deerfield Academy
Deerfield, MA 01342
(800) 723-7704

Cosmos Soccer Camps
Soccer Camps of America, Inc.
Ramapo College
505 Ramapo Valley Road
Mahwah, NJ 07430
(201) 529-7500

Pine Tree Soccer Camp
Lynn University
P.O. Box 267
Fourth Lake
Inlet, NY 13360
(315) 369-3680

Tennis

4 Star Tennis Academy
P.O. Box 3387
Salls Church, VA 22043
(800) 334-7827

Nick Bollettieri Tennis Camps
5550 34 Street West
Braddenton, FL 34210
(800) USA-NICK

Future Stars Tennis Camps
P.O. Box 965
Quogue, NY 11959
(516) 653-6767

The Lawrenceville Tennis Camp
The Lawrenceville School
Lawrenceville, NJ 08648
(609) 896-0054

Menominee Tennis Camp
4985 Highway D
Eagle River, WI 54521
(800) 236-CAMP

Offense-Defense Tennis Camp
(Curry College)
Judy and Mike Meshken
P.O. Box 11
Easton, CT 06612
(800) TENNIS-3

Sabin-Mulloy-Garrison Tennis Camp
11550 Lastchance Road
Clermont, FL 34711
(352) 394-3543

Saddlebrook International Tennis
5700 Saddlebrook Way
Wesley Chapel, FL 33543
(800) 729-8383

Track and Field

Bates College Track and Field Camp
Bates College
Office of Summer Programs
Lewiston, ME 04240
(207) 786-6077

Craftsbury Running Camp
Craftsbury Sports Center
Box 31
Craftsbury Common, VT 05827
(800) 729-7751

Volleyball

Vassar College Summer Volleyball
Camp
Vassar College
Poughkeepsie, NY 12601
(914) 437-5900

Water Sports

Camp Normandie
Furnace Point Road
Westport, NY 12993
(800) 206-8333

International Program
SFU International Exchange
Sports For Understanding (SFU)
3501 Newark Street, NW
Washington, DC 20016
(800) 424-3691

Kutscher's Sports Academy
Anawana Lake
Monticello, NY 12701
(800) 724-0238

Baseball, Basketball and Soccer Camps
2546 Cropsey Avenue
Brooklyn, NY 11214
(718) 946-9827 or
(201) 691-0070

**Other College and University
Programs**
American University
4400 Massachusetts Avenue, NW
Washington, DC 20016
* The AU Field Hockey Camp: (202)
  885-3018
* The AU Girls' Basketball Camp:
  (202) 885-3023
* The AU School of Swimming: (202)
  885-3080
* The AU Soccer Camp: (202) 885-3014
* The AU Wrestling Camp:
  (202) 885-3000
* The Capitol Boys' Basketball Camp:
  (202) 885-3000
* The H.E.A.T., Inc. Tennis Camp:
  (202) 885-3017

Babson College
150 Great Plain Avenue
Wellesley, MA 02181
(617) 235-1200

Bates College AU—Sports Camp
Bates College
Office of Summer Programs
Lewiston, ME 04240
(207) 786-6077

Cortland Summer Sports Schools
SUNY College at Cortland
P.O. Box 2000
Cortland, NY 13045
(607) 753-4960

Franklin and Marshall Sports Camp
Franklin and Marshall College
P.O. Box 3003
Lancaster, PA 17604
(717) 291-4106

Giezholz Institute for Lifelong Learning
Ferris State University (FSU)
Big Rapids, MI 49307
(616) 592-2211

* FSU Girls' Junior Varsity, Varsity, and
  Position Basketball Camps
* FSU Golf Camp
* FSU Summer Hockey School
* FSU Tennis Academy
* FSU Volleyball Training Camp

Hartwick College Sports Camps
Hartwick College
Oneonta, NY 13820
(607) 431-4700

IUP Summer Sports Camps
Indiana U of Pennsylvania
Field House
Indiana, PA 15705
(412) 357-2757

Ithaca College Sports Camps
Continuing Education and Summer Sessions
Ithaca College
953 Danbury Road
Ithaca, NY 14850
(607) 274-3143

Mercersburg Summer Sports Programs
The Mercersburg Academy
Mercersburg, PA 17236
(717) 328-3851

Miami University Summer Sports
  Schools
Miami University
220 Millet Hall
Oxford, OH 45056
(513) 529-2472

NMU Summer Sports Camps
Northern Michigan University
Athletic Department
Marquette, MI 49855
(800) 553-7817

Odessa College Sports Camp
Odessa College
201 West University
Odessa, TX 79764
(915) 335-6348 or X6688

Ohio University Sports Camps
Ohio University
Athens, OH 45701
(800) 336-5699

Penn State Sports Camps
Penn State University
123 Keller Building
University Park, PA 16802
(814) 865-0561

Pfeiffer College Summer Athletic
Program
Pfeiffer College
Misenheimer, NC 28109
(800) 338-2060

Princeton University Sports Camps
Princeton University
Center for Visitors and Conference Services
71 University Place
Princeton, NJ 08544-2088
(609) 258-1900

Shippensburg University Sports Camps
Shippensburg University of
Pennsylvania
1871 Old Main Drive
Shippensburg, PA 17257
(717) 532-1256

SLU Summer Sports Schools
St. Lawrence University
Carlton, NY 13617
(315) 379-5883

University of San Diego Sports Camp
University of Sand Diego Sports Center
Alcala Park 5998
San Diego, CA 92110
(619) 260-4593

University of Wisconsin at Green Bay
Summer Sport Camp
University of WI at Green Bay
Office of Outreach and Extension
Green Bay, WI 54311-7001
(414) 465-2145

When contacting these organizations, ask for a description of the programs, facilities, faculty, schedules, admissions policies, and costs. You can find additional companies and organizations sponsoring athletic camps and membership activities for high school students through the Internet sites listed at the end of this chapter.

THE COLLEGE CONNECTION

When a student applies to college, admissions officers will look at her extracurricular record to determine whether she can become a positive, contributing member of their society. They'll look to see whether she has participated in a wide range of activities and therefore is likely to be a well-rounded person. They will also look to see where she has distinguished herself: in scholarship, the arts, on the athletic field, through leadership, or some other area. Colleges and universities look for interesting, tolerant, well-rounded, and active individuals with special interests and skills. Can your child demonstrate a depth (i.e., intensity) and breadth (i.e., diversity) of experiences in your extracurricular activities? Is he a scholar, athlete, or special talent? The more categories he can genuinely check off, the more attractive he is to admissions officers.

Competitive colleges look for students who bring a unique perspective or skill to their schools. It helps if an admissions committee can look to your child's activities and answer "yes" to the following:

- Does he actively pursue his interests?
- Does she build on existing or develop new skills?
- Is she a good team player? Able to get along with others?
- Is he interested in helping others?
- Has he demonstrated a commitment to your community?
- Has he excelled in academics, the arts, or on the athletic field?
- Is she outgoing? Intelligent? Mature?
- Has she exhibited leadership skills?
- Does she possess unique skills and interests?

As your child develops a unique and rich set of experiences (and is able to answer "yes" to all of these questions) he will find that he in great demand from the schools looking for accomplished individuals.

HOW EXTRACURRICULARS ARE EVALUATED BY COLLEGES

College admissions committees are not just providing lip service in their attempts to attract well-rounded students. They actively incorporate these goals into their application for admissions. Here's one example: The Admissions Committee for Harvard and Radcliffe Colleges states, "we are keenly interested in attracting and admitting candidates who show evidence of such personal qualities as honesty, fairness, compassion, altruism, leadership and initiative in their high school years...." Furthermore, the application for Harvard/Radcliffe includes a "General Ratings" form for extracurricular activities. The content of this ratings form is shown below:

HARVARD/RADCLIFFE COLLEGES
GENERAL RATINGS FORM

"In making the following ratings please compare this student with his or her entire secondary school class. Please check the single most appropriate box for each item."

Criteria	Average or below Average	Good (above Average)	Excellent (Top 10% this year)	Outstanding (top 5% this year)	One of the top few I have ever encountered in my career
Academic motivation					
Academic creativity					
Academic self-discipline					
Academic growth potential					
Leadership					
Self-confidence					
Warmth of personality					
Sense of humor					
Concern for others					
Energy and enthusiasm					
Emotional maturity					
Personal initiative					
Reaction to setbacks					
Respect accorded by faculty					

All competitive schools ask about extracurricular activities. They are not looking for a laundry list of activities, but they do want to see what a student perceives to be his more important talents and accomplishments. Becoming an active member in an organization or activity will get your child the most out of the activity and will look most appealing to colleges when it's time to apply.

SUMMARY

High school is a time for fun, exploration, learning, personal growth, and travel; extracurricular activities are one important way for a young person to learn more about himself and the world. By participating in extracurriculars, not only will your teen gain personally through her contributions to the community around her, but she will have an opportunity to build an impressive résumé that will demonstrate her character and skills to her target schools.

To help you and your child plan and organize his extracurricular activities, check out the Extracurricular Activities Tracking Sheet on Kaplan's Web site at www.kaplan.com/downloads/.

TELL YOUR TEEN

* Undertake at least one self-study project during your high school years.

* Get involved in at least two extracurricular activities each academic year.

* Consider an activity that will take place outside of your community.

INTERNET RESOURCES

Academic Interests

Astro Web: Astronomy/Astrophysics on the Internet.
http://fits.cv.nrao.edu/www/astronomy.html
Collection of pointers to astronomy-related information available on the Internet.

Chemistry. http://www.chem.ucla.edu/chempointers.html
Collection of pointers to chemistry resources on the Internet.

Explore Net. http://www.exploratorium.edu/
Collection of electronic science exhibits and resources for students.

MasterCard's Student Page. http://www.mastercard.com/students/
Links to academic area-related sites on the Internet.

Physics. http://www/yahoo.com/science/physics
Collection of pointers to physics resources on the Internet.

SchoolNet. http://www.schoolnet.org/
Active discussion of issues from violence in schools to the concerns of college-bound students.

Science Education Center. http://www.llnl.gov/sci_educ/nesp.html
This site, sponsored by the National Education Supercomputer Program, provides instructional materials and tools in science and mathematics.

Public Service

American Express' Student Page. http://www.americanexpress.com/student
For up-to-date links to jobs and internships with nonprofit organizations.

Boy Scouts of America. http://www.bsa.scouting.org
Community, citizenship, and self-reliance issues and tips.

Environmental Learning Center. http://www.nptn.org/cyber.serv/aonep/academy_one/learn/menu.environ.html.
Examine and discuss environmental issues.

Rainforest Action Network. http://www.ran.org/ran
Information on efforts to protect the world's rainforests.

RedRibbonNet. http://www.redribbon.net
Information on HIV and AIDS education, research and related initiatives.

Special Interests

Agudas Achim. http://uscj.org/seabd/alexanaa/agcoll.html
Place to learn about Jewish life and community issues.

Arts Edge. http://artsedge.kennedy-center.org/
Links to information and resources on the arts. Includes an online showcase for young artists.

KidNews. http://www.vsa.cape.com/~powens/Kidnews3.html
An international student newspaper.

Guide to Museums and other Cultural Resources on the Web.
http://www.lam.mus.ca.us/webmuseums
Pick a destination, from around the world, for a listing of resources.

Online Magazines. http://place.scholastic.com/classmag/index.htm
Online magazine featuring student writers, poets, and journalists.

Scholastic Network. http://www.scholastic.com
Participate in contests, try out subject-based activities, and communicate with researchers on expeditions, worldwide, online.

Street Cents. http://www.screen.com/streetcents.html
Online magazine on consumer issues written by and for students.

The Student Center. http://www.infomall.org:80/studentcenter/
Information, news, services, and other activities for students.

Student Press. http://studentpress.journ.umn.edu/
A warehouse of journalism-related links for students.

Teen Mania Ministries. http://www.teenmania.org
Information on Christian programs and interest groups.

Sports-Related Sites

All Sport Recruiting Coordinators. http://www.webcreations.com/allsport
Commercial site that provides information on locating college coaches and qualifying for athletic scholarships.

The Athlete's Diary. http://www.stevenscreek.com/
Commercial site with demonstration software of a multisport computer log and diary, books, calculators, and other tools for athletes.

College Bound Student-Athletes. http://www.in.net/cbsa
Commercial site with books, videos, and other services for sale to student-athletes and their parents.

College Sports Recruiting Network. http://www.cbsa.org
This site intends to introduce high school athletes from around the world to U.S. college and university coaches.

Do It Sports. http://www.doitsports.com
Results, race entries, and course maps for athletes in many outdoor sports.

Femina. http://www.femina.com/femina/sports
Links to women's sports pages.

Fitness-Related Web Sites. http://www.montana.com/stafford/fitnesslinks.html
Links to sites on fitness and fitness-related topics, such as exercise, health, nutrition, and medicine.

Forrest Davis Football Recruiting. http://www.forrestdavis.com/
A leading college football recruiting analyst provides information on his services as well as searchable bios on top recruiting prospects.

Kidscamps—Sports Camps. http://www.kidscamps.com/specialty/sports
Listing of sports camps.

Multisport School of Champions. http://www.multisports.com
Intensive training camp for athletes of all levels.

National Scouting Report—Online Recruiting Center. http://www.nsr-inc.com
Commercial service with an online searchable database of high school student athletes.

Prep Illustrated. http://www.netins.net/showcase/sports
Online magazine devoted entirely to high school sports.

Road Runners of America. http://www.rrca.org
News, events, membership information, programs and services, publications, and an online forum for runners.

SPORT A.S.I.S.T. http://www.athletes.com/asist.html
Commercial site with information and books for sale to student-athletes and their parents.

Sportsworld. http://www.sportsworld.com/
Source of world-wide sports information, merchandise, and competition results (both amateur and professional).

t@p online. http://www.taponline.com
Links to college athletic clubs, college team home pages, and college team standings.

Study- and Travel-Abroad Listings

Foreign Exchange Programs
American Field Service (AFS). http://www.afs.org/
Info on AFS opportunities for intercultural learning, including program listings and a "global classroom."

American Institute for Foreign Study (AIFS). http://www.aifs.org/
Listings or work- or study-related cultural exchange programs.

AYUSA Study Abroad. http://www.ayusa.com
International exchange programs for high school students.

Council Travel. http://www.ciee.org/
Travel discounts, job opportunities, volunteer projects, student exchange programs, and more.

Cultural Homestay International (CHI). http://www.chinet.org
Short-term "homestay" and academic programs for students from 34 countries.

FSL Languages Around the World. http://www.access.digex.net/~greybarn
Placements with host families, high school and college programs, and English language coursework.

High School Programs in Israel. http://shamash.org/reform
Info on religious and secular high school programs in Israel.

National Registration Center for Study Abroad (NRCSA).
http://www.nrcsa.com/index.html
Program and course finders for students of all ages.

Online Study-Abroad Directory. http://www.istc.umn.edu/
Hundreds of study abroad programs.

Peterson's. http://www.petersons.com/summerop/ssector.html
Summer programs for kids and teenagers.

Pacific International Exchange. http://www.pieusa.org/become_passport_student.html

"Passport" program for American teens.
studyabroad.com! http://www.studyabroad.com
Online study-abroad information resource for exchange programs, summer programs, internships, and intensive language courses.

Youth Exchange Services. http://www.yesint.com
Opportunities for teenage exchange students.

Youth For Understanding (YFU). http://www.yfu.org
Information on becoming an exchange student, host family, or volunteer.

Language Programs:
Center for Languages and Latin American Studies.
http://www.tnl-online.com/cllas/cllas.htm
Spanish language school in Mexico with live-in immersion programs for students and professionals.

E. F. Language Travel. http://www.ef.com/
Language teaching, educational travel, and cultural exchange.

Eurocentres. http://www.clark.net/pub/eurocent/
Listing of schools around the world that offer language study and cultural exchange.

Foreign Language Study-Abroad Service (FLSAS).
http://www.netpoint.net/~flsas/
Information on intensive language programs in other countries.

Intel Cross. http://www.study-abroad.org/
International programs to meet "most everybody's needs."

NRCSA Language Program for Teens.
http://www.urcsa.com/teenprograms/index.html
List of teen programs at schools around the world.

Summer Culture and Language Experiences (S.C.A.L.E.).
http://www.princeton.edu/~peterp/scale.html
Directory of opportunities for children to learn about other societies.

Summer Camp Directories and Programs:
Camp and Conference Home Page. http://www.camping.org
A directory of camps, conferences, retreats, and outdoor education programs.

Camp Channel. http://www.campchannel.com
Search engine for camps, a home shopping center for camp needs, and more.

Camper's Collection. http://www.kidscamps.com/marketplace/campers-collection
A conglomeration of products designed for campers.

Earthwatch. http://www.earthwatch.org/
College courses for credit from Drexel University in subjects ranging from Animal Behavior to Wildlife Management.

Intensive Wilderness Adventure Program.
http://www.neobahn.com.mtyr/iwap.html
Adventure programs with offer training in wilderness skills and environmental awareness.

Kids' Camps. http://www.kidscamps.com
A comprehensive directory of camps and summer experiences.

National Camp Association. http://www.summercamp.org
Personalized guidance and referrals to residential camps and summer programs

Rhode Island School of Design. http://www.risd.edu/sumrsite/sumrhome.html
Or e-mail at: summer@risd.edu
Summer offerings at RISD.

Worldwide Camp Directory. http://www.wwcamp.com/
Online services devoted to the world of camping.

Travel Resources:
American Youth Hostels.
http://www.taponline.com/tap/travel/hostels/pages/hosthp.htm
Listings of hostelling locations around the world. Additional information on membership, reservations, and publications.

Center for Disease Control. http://www.cdc.gov/travel/travel.html
Information on vaccine requirements, food and water precautions, and recommendations by geographic regions.

City.Net. http://www.city.net/
The most comprehensive international guide to communities around the world. Updated daily, it provides easy and timely access to information on travel, entertainment, and local business and government activity.

U.S. Information Agency. http://www.usia.gov
Extensive information on international travel and exchange activities.

U.S. State Department Travel Advisories. http://travel.state.gov
Information about getting or renewing passports, consular notes about foreign countries, and travel warnings and announcements.

CHAPTER 5

Work

WHAT STUDENTS ASK

- **How do I find a job?**
- **What businesses can I start on my own?**
- **Where can I find career information?**

There are many reasons why high school students work, ranging from contributing to the family income to exploring a potential career. Whatever the motivation, working while in high school can help your child boost her chances of getting into her target colleges, since holding down a job while going to school shows initiative and organization. In addition, students learn work skills like showing up on time, following directions, getting along with coworkers, and managing money—all skills that come in handy throughout life. Finally, if your child explores career interests while still in high school, he may be more likely to choose the right college, and make the most of his college years.

DEVELOPING WORK SKILLS

Your child is developing work-related skills while attending high school. Here are a few examples.

WORK SKILLS	
Skill	**Goal**
Attendance	Show up.
Complete assignments	Only make promises you can keep, and keep those you make.
Initiative	Participate actively in the classroom. Ask questions.
Punctuality	Get to your classes on time.
Working with others	Seek out opportunities to work with other students. Try to join a team sport.

WORK ISSUES

What does your child want from a job? Is it money? Experience? A career boost? Depending on his needs, he may choose to volunteer his time, work for pay, or start his own business. To help your child find the right work experience, have him think about his goals as well as the following issues:

- Is pay important? Necessary?
- When can you work? During the school year, holiday seasons, summer, or year-round?
- What are your skills and talents?
- What are your interests?
- Do you want to work for others or would you like to work for yourself?

His answers to these questions can help the two of you identify his needs and target the work that is right for him. If money is not a key consideration, then your child's opportunities increase greatly; there are nonpaying internships and volunteer positions in business and community groups that can provide experience to develop and apply the key work skills. Is your daughter interested in term-time, holiday, summer, or year-round employment? Her availability will influence the kind of job she can take. For example, if she is loaded down with extracurriculars, a summer job may be her best option.

FINDING A JOB

Your teen's first step in finding a job should be checking out legal issues. There are employment laws that control when, where, and how many hours students under

18 may work, as well as the minimum wage that they are able to earn. Some of these laws vary by state and region. To find out more about these rules, and to determine which ones affect you, contact the guidance or local employment office. While you are getting information on these employment laws, you may want to help your son get a social security card, working papers, and a driver's license, if he doesn't already have them. These papers can make it easier to get started once he's found a job.

Once your daughter has the necessary paperwork, she's ready to begin her job search. What follows are some of the potential sources for work for high school students.

Classified ad section of the local newspaper. Look through the Help Wanted section of your local newspaper. Pay particular attention to the sections for part-time and summer jobs.

Community bulletin boards. Some small-business owners advertise positions where motivated students, or their parents, are found, like the local YMCA. Investigate these community centers to see if jobs are posted on their bulletin boards.

Cultural sites. Museums and theaters are excellent sources of term-time and summer work. Visit these sites and ask about ushering, ticket sales, clerical, and other job opportunities.

Large companies. These companies—telephone, gas, electric and water utilities, insurance companies, banks and law offices—often sponsor summer jobs and unpaid internships. Have your teen write to the Human Resources department of companies she's interested in and ask about job opportunities.

Local businesses. Most high school students work in community-based small businesses like grocery stores, dry cleaners, stationery and office supply stores, fast food outlets, restaurants, clothing outlets, and bookstores. Encourage your son to take an afternoon and walk around the mall or local business districts, and ask the business owners or managers if they are hiring.

Local colleges and universities. If there is a large college or university in your area, you may want to contact the Human Resource department for summer jobs. Although these schools scale back their programs during the summer, they may need to fill in for vacationing students and staff.

Local hospitals. Hospitals are a great source for unpaid internships during the school year and summer. (This may be an especially appropriate for a student considering a career in medicine, nursing or public health). Write or visit the Human Resource department of your local hospital and ask about internship opportunities.

Summer camps. Each year thousands of summer camps hire high school students as counselors and activity coordinators. Contact the camps in your area or consult the camps listed in chapters four and five.

Town offices. Your town's Department of Health, Parks Department, Visitor's Bureau, or Chamber of Commerce may set aside funds to hire students for summer work. Check your local phonebook—it probably has a separate section for local government listings.

Cooperative education or employment office. Many schools, particularly in large cities, have a cooperative education or career counseling office to help you find a job. While most of the jobs are for the school year, some summer jobs may also exist. Contact your guidance office to determine whether these services exist at your high school.

People you know. You or your friends may know about job opportunities, and may be in a position to offer your son a job or direct him to someone who is hiring.

Job Search Tips

There are a number of things that a teenager needs to do in seeking out a job. Help her by offering the following guidelines:

- Know yourself: Figure out where you'd ideally like to work and what you'd like to do. Even if your dream job isn't available, trying for it might lead you to other possibilities.
- Prepare a résumé that includes your:
  - Name, address, and phone number
  - Educational background (including the name of your high school, expected year of graduation, cumulative grade point average, and relevant extracurricular activities)
  - Employment background (including period of employment, name of company, position, and a brief description of your responsibilities and accomplishments)
  - Special skills and interests (including foreign languages and computer skills)

- List of references (including names and telephone numbers)
- On interviews, make sure you:
  - Get there on time
  - Wear appropriate clothes (no jeans, sneakers, or outrageously funky outfits)
  - Speak clearly (no gum chewing)
  - Speak standard English
  - Maintain eye contact with your interviewer

Finally, once you have completed your interview, remember to thank the interviewer and follow up your meeting with a thank-you note.

JOB ALTERNATIVES

If your teenager has entrepreneurial leanings, she may be interested in creating her own job. Starting her own business means she can work her own hours and meet other commitments, make money while assuming more responsibility and risk, or sell a product or service that is in short supply.

Entrepreneurial Activities

What are some of the businesses a teen can start on his own? Here are descriptions of 16 jobs that he can do in his spare time. Almost all of these opportunities require very little money and time to begin.

Audiovisual services. People are always looking for ways to record special occasions like birthdays, bridal showers, and weddings without having to do it themselves. If your child has access to home video equipment and can operate some of the special functions like laying titles and editing, he may want to look into this opportunity.

Babysitting. Is your daughter responsible, energetic, and good with kids? If so, then this may be the perfect job for her. Help her decide on a rate, then pass the word around to people you know.

Car wash. She can put together a flyer announcing her services and stick it under car windshields.

Computer installation. Lots of people buy computers but don't know how to assemble and operate them. If your daughter is familiar with computers, can follow instructions well, and is able to demonstrate these skills to others, she may want to go after this opportunity. She may be able to advertise at a local computer store.

Custodial services. Many adults would rather pay someone to clean their homes than do it themselves. Cleaning houses can mean good money and a chance to work independently. A related business is recycling papers, plastics, and cans. Teens can earn money while cleaning up the environment a bit.

Delivery/messenger service. There is always a need for someone to run errands, deliver newspapers, or shop and deliver groceries. Depending on your area, your son will need sturdy shoes and a bicycle, moped, or motorcycle.

Desktop publishing. If she's creative, has design software for her personal computer, and would like to try her hand at creating newsletters or marketing materials for school activities, local businesses, and community-based groups, she may want to consider desktop publishing. Encourage her to design a great-looking flyer listing the services she offers—it's a sample of her work.

Lawn mowing. Lots of cash, a chance to work in the great outdoors, and exercise galore. Or invest in a shovel to help your neighbors out of the snow.

Merchandising. Gear is in—caps, water bottles, key chains, T-shirts, jerseys, and other paraphernalia to promote a team or event. The hitch is that you need capital (money) to start a venture like this. But the demand and potential to make money with an idea is big.

Painting. You don't need lots of capital here—all you need are paint brushes, dust covers, and lots of energy and patience.

Promoting. Is your son an organizational maverick? Does he have an eye for detail? He may want to consider sponsoring a local event like a small concert, race, or other contest. The work here may include advertising sales, ticket sales, local business sponsorships, and merchandising opportunities.

Publications. With fewer dollars being put into extracurricular activities, many schools find themselves without key student publications. Teens can turn this into opportunity by publishing school calendars, team posters, school handbook, or student directories. The biggest challenge is figuring out the publication that is most needed and then gathering the information for it. Most of these publications can be produced with the use of a personal computer and a printer. Your child can earn money selling individual copies and by selling ads to local businesses.

Self-made items. If your child has a particular talent in making objects, she may want to begin selling them. Whether it's cakes, clothing, or artwork, she may be able to sell her wares through local stores or craft fairs.

Software installation and training. Does he know his wordprocessing or spreadsheet software like the back of his hand? Not everyone does. He can start a business of installing and training home users on the more popular software packages.

Tutoring. How can your teen capitalize on his straight A's in math while helping others? Teach! Patience and the ability to communicate clearly are key skills for this line of work. His area of expertise doesn't have to be academic: He can help people boost their athletic or music skills as well.

Word-processing. Lots of students need their papers typed but don't have the hardware. Your daughter can establish a service typing school papers and résumés for students and others in your community.

Many of these jobs require you to market your services with a flyer to get the word out. You can distribute flyers under car windshields, in mail boxes, on bulletin boards in supermarkets, laundromats, schools, and libraries, and door-to-door. Your might want to check what information (phone, e-mail address, etcetera) your son or daughter is planning to give out before he or she starts advertising.

Setting Limits

Make sure your child doesn't become too wrapped up in his work. Juggling work with other responsibilities takes a lot of concentration and effort. Remember, school work should come first, no matter how much he enjoys his job. Most students can readily handle jobs that require up to ten hours of work a week. If your child is active in other extracurricular activities it will be hard for her to devote more time than this. If her work becomes too much, encourage her to talk to her employer about modifying her schedule or cutting back her hours.

RESEARCHING CAREERS

You may want to help your teenager look for a job that is an entree to a career. One way of learning about different lines of work is by consulting books that explore different career opportunities. The most popular of these books is probably the U.S. govern-

> "Work has given me something else to challenge me, something that isn't quite as stressful as school."
>
> —High school senior

ment's *Occupational Outlook Handbook*. This is published biannually and provides information on careers, including training and educational requirements, the type of work done, starting salaries, related jobs, and more. He can also contact some of the many professional organizations that provide information on careers, scholarships, and colleges offering programs in their industries. A listing of organizations in popular fields is provided below.

Accounting
American Institute of Certified Public Accountants
1211 Avenue of the Americas
New York, NY 10036

Acting and Directing
National Association of Schools of Theater
11250 Roger Bacon Drive, Suite 21
Reston, VA 22090

Advertising
American Advertising Federation
1101 Vermont Avenue, NW
Suite 500
Washington, DC 20005

Aerospace
Aerospace Education Foundation
1501 Lee Highway
Arlington, VA 22209

Anthropology
American Anthropological Association
4350 North Fairfax Drive, Suite 640
Arlington, VA 22203

Archaeology
Society for American Archaeology
900 2nd Street, NE, #12
Washington, DC 20022

Architecture
Director, Careers in Architecture Program
The American Institute of Architects
1735 New York Avenue, NW
Washington, DC 20006

Banking
American Bankers Association
1120 Connecticut Avenue, NW
Washington, DC 20036

Biology
American Institute of Biological Sciences
Education Division
730 11th Street, NW
Washington, DC 20001

Chemistry
American Chemical Society
Career Services
1155 16th Street, NW
Washington, DC 20036

Computer Programming
Institute for the Certification of Computer Professionals
2200 East Devon Avenue, Suite 268
Des Plaines, IL 60018

Dance and Choreography
National Dance Association
1900 Association Drive
Reston, VA 22091

Dentistry
SELECT Program
Department of Career Guidance
American Dental Association
211 East Chicago Avenue
Chicago, IL 60611

Diet and Nutrition
The American Dietetic Association
216 West Jackson Boulevard
Chicago, IL 60606

Economics
American Economic Association
2014 Broadway, Suite 305
Nashville, TN 37205

Engineering
JETS—Guidance
1420 King Street, Suite 405
Alexandria, VA 22314
Financial Management
Financial Managers Society
85 Michigan Avenue, Suite 500
Chicago, IL 60603

General Management
American Management Association
2210 Arbor Boulevard
Dayton, OH 45439

Geography
Association of American Geographers
1710 16 Street, NW
Washington, DC 20009

Geology
American Geological Institute
4220 King Street
Alexandria, VA 22302

Graphic Design
National Association of Schools of Art
& Design
11250 Roger Bacon Drive, Suite 21
Reston, VA 22090

History
Organization of American Historians
112 North Bryant Street
Bloomington, IN 47408

Hotel and Restaurant Management
Council on Hotel, Restaurant,
and Institutional Education
1200 17 Street, NW
Washington, DC 20036

Interior Design
American Society of Interior Designers
Student Affairs Coordinator
608 Massachusetts Avenue, NE
Washington, DC 20002

Law
American Bar Association
541 North Fairbanks Court
Chicago, IL 60611

Management Analysts and Consultants
The Association of Management
Consulting Firms
521 Fifth Avenue, 35th Floor
New York, NY 10017

Marketing
American Marketing Association
250 South Wacker Drive
Chicago, IL 60606

Mathematics
American Mathematical Society
P.O. Box 6248
Providence, RI 02940

Medicine
American Medical Association
Division of Undergraduate Medical
Education
515 North State Street
Chicago, IL 60610

Meteorology
American Meteorological Society
45 Beacon Street
Boston, MA 02108

Military
U.S. Military Entrance Processing
Command
Careers in the Military
2500 Green Bay Road
North Chicago, IL 60064

Music
National Association of Schools of Music
11250 Roger Bacon Drive, Suite 21
Reston, VA 22091

Nursing
American Association of Colleges
of Nursing
1 Dupont Circle, Suite 530
Washington, DC 20036

Optometry
American Optometric Association
Educational Services
243 North Lindberg Boulevard
St. Louis, MO 63141

Pharmacy
American Association of Colleges of
Pharmacy
1426 Prince Street
Alexandria, VA 22314

Physical Education
National Association for Sport and
Physical Education
1900 Association Drive
Reston, VA 22091

Physical Therapy
1111 North Fairfax Street
Alexandria, VA 22314

Physics
American Institute of Physics
One Physics Ellipse
College Park, MD 20740

Political Science
American Political Science Association
1527 New Hampshire Avenue, NW
Washington, DC 20036

Production (Industrial)
American Manufacturing Association
135 West 50th Street
New York, NY 10020

Public Relations
Public Relations Society of America, Inc.
Educational Affairs Department
33 Irving Place, Third Floor
New York, NY 10003

Purchasing and Buying (Retail)
National Retail Federation
100 West 31 Street
New York, NY 10001

Real Estate
National Association of Realtors
777 14th Street, NW
Washington, DC 20005

Religion
Association of Theological Schools
10 Summit Drive
Pittsburgh, PA 15275

Social Work
Council on Social Work
1600 Duke Street
Alexandria, VA 22314

Sociology
American Sociological Association
1722 N Street, NW
Washington, DC 20036

Teaching
American Federation of Teachers
555 New Jersey Avenue, NW
Washington, DC 20001

Travel
American Society of Travel Agents
Education Department
1101 King Street, Suite 200
Alexandria, VA 22314

Veterinary Medicine
American Veterinary Medical
Association
1931 North Meacham Road, Suite 100
Schaumburg, IL 60173

Volunteer Work
Peace Corps of the U.S.A.
Information Office
1990 K Street, NW
Washington, DC 20526

IN-SCHOOL OPPORTUNITIES

There are other ways to learn more about specific careers. One option is to attend a career-based magnet school. These academies are focused on specific industries like business, nursing, media, and teaching. Often these schools combine classes with internships, and in this way, the material presented in class can be applied directly to work. They also provide exposure to careers through field trips, guest teachers, and special projects. If your daughter has has a specific career interest in mind, explore your area for special schools and programs that target her industry or occupation of interest. She can also look into the following opportunities to learn more about careers:

- Join business and career clubs at school.
- Interview family and friends about their jobs, asking about what they do, how they got started, their qualifications, and how much they make (ask this one discreetly).

- Attend career fairs. Ask employers about job opportunities, educational requirements, and their industry's prospects for the future.
- Go on field trips to local business to see and ask about jobs first-hand.
- Get online and browse the many Internet-related sites on finding out the jobs that are right for you, searching for specific jobs, and looking up industries and companies. The sites listed at the end of this chapter can provide you with a good start.

DO IT NOW!

Don't underestimate the importance of helping your child learn about careers while still in high school. Some career paths have an impact on the courses he should take in high school and the major he should select in college. Here's an example of how a specific interest can work to influence choice of colleges and courses.

CAREER/INDUSTRY →	COLLEGE MAJOR →	HIGH SCHOOL COURSES
Advertising	Business Administration Marketing Journalism	English (4 years) Art (1 year)
Chemical Engineering	Chemical Engineering Chemistry Engineering	Math (through calculus) Science (including Chemistry and Physics)
Teaching (Elementary Education)	Child Psychology Education	Psychology and Sociology English (including classes in Communication)

Obviously, his choice of career can also influence the college he targets. Just like high schools, some colleges are better equipped to train for particular careers than others. For example, a student interested in graphic arts would probably consider an art institute over her local college. Bear in mind that a "top" school in one area is not necessarily a top school in other areas. Help your son identify at least three careers that interests him. Help him find out all he can about these careers including the colleges and universities that can best prepare him for them.

SUMMARY

The key to getting a job, landing an internship, or starting your own business is initiative. Without it the other guys willing to send out letters, knock on doors, and promote their services will get the work. Colleges are looking for students who demonstrate initiative, and for good reason: at college, success depends on how well you motivate yourself to choose the right classes, attend them, complete your homework, and join in extracurricular activities. Your teenager also needs to get a head start applying other job-related skills to her everyday life. These skills include learning to follow directions, work well with others, complete what she begins, and be responsible with her time and money. As your son plans his high school years, he should also find opportunities to work and to learn about careers. His career interest may have implications for his high school plan of study and choice of colleges.

TELL YOUR TEEN

* Commit to at least one work experience during high school.
* Limit your work commitment to no more than 15 hours a week during the school year.
* Try to find a balance between work and other commitments.

INTERNET RESOURCES

Career Resources

CareerWeb. http://www.cweb.com/homepage.html
Career interest inventory and a library of career reference materials.

The Catapult on the Web. http://www.jobweb.org/catapult/catapult.htm
The spring-board to career- and job-related sites, including helpful career guides and a library of career resources.

The Indiana College Placement and Assessment Center.
http://bronze.ucs.indiana.edu/~gillies/home.html
Education and career guidance information.

Occupational Information Network. http://www.doleta.gov/programs/onet
Electronic directory and description of occupational titles.

Outdoor Environmental Career Guides.
http://www.princeton.edu/~oa.html#outdoor &environmental
Job resource guide on outdoor and environmental careers given to students at Princeton University.

Occupational Outlook. http://stats.bls.gov/ocohome.html
Provides a copy of the Occupational Outlook Handbook, a comprehensive listing of occupations, including salary information, projected demands, and training required.

America's Job Bank. http://www.ajb.dni.us
A site containing the largest number of active job opportunities in the world.

Americorps. http://www.Americorps.org
Earn money for college while helping others in the community.

Jobs

ETA Youth Training Programs. http://doleta.gov/programs/youthtrn.htm
Information on summer and year-round employment programs; one-stop career center; job corps; and, apprenticeship training for youth.

Minority High School Apprentice Program.
http://web.fie.com/web/fed/doe/success/succs235.htm
Information on an eight-week internship program that places students from underrepresented groups (Black, Hispanic, native American, and Pacific Islander) into one-on-one relationships with Brookhaven National Laboratory scientists engaged in health-related research.

National Science Center. http://www.acq.osd.mil/ddre/edugate/eeepgm.html#nsc
Cooperative education experience designed to introduce career opportunities in science and math to high school students.

Peterson's. http://www.petersons.com
For listings of summer jobs and other programs for high school students.

Job Search

College Board Online. http://www.collegeboard.org
Explore careers and college majors.

Espan. http://www.espan.com/js/ref/oohand.html
online employment connection, with links to job search, career, and HR resources.

Loci. http://www.Loci.com/
See the Breaking into the Real World section where you can review Loci's 8-step job search guide.

The Social Security Administration. http://www.ssa.gov/
On-line forms available.

Big Businesses

Aetna (Insurance). http://www.aetna.com
This insurance company provides information on job opportunities, plus a "what's new" section with current events.

American Airlines (Transportation). http://www.americanair.com/
Travel tips, contests, and career info from one of the country's largest airlines.

American Express (Financial Services). http://americanexpress.com/student
A Web resource for college students, with everything from movie reviews to credit card application forms.

Andersen Consulting. http://www.ac.com
This global management and technology consulting organization's home page offers tips on career opportunities.

Apple Computers. http://www.apple.com/
The makers of Macintosh computers provide news, contests, and a directory of new products.

AT&T (Telecommunications). http://www.att.com/
Directory of telecommunications services, a "brain spin" interactive site, and resources for kids.

Chrysler (Automotive). http://www.chryslercorp.com/
Learn about cars, education, the environment, careers, and more at this home page.

Citibank (Financial Services). http://www.citicorp.com
Job postings for Citibank positions.

Coca-Cola (Beverages). http://www.cocacola.com/
Get some "mental refreshment" at this cool site.

Delta Airlines (Transportation). http://www.delta-air.com
Delta news and flight information.

Disney (Entertainment). http://www.disney.com
Experience the world of Disney, or order products from this site.

Dow Chemical Company. http://www.dow.com/
Info on Dow products and services and the industries Dow serves.

DuPont (Chemicals). http://www.dupont.com
Focus on DuPont products, environmental and health concerns, and job opportunities.

FedEx (Shipping). http://www.fedex.com
online services, career info, learning labs, and free software from this site.

Ford (Automotive). http://www.ford.com/
This site connects to home pages all over the world.

General Motors (Automotive). http://www.gm.com
Info on GM prodoucts, plus interactive educational sites and a concepts lab previewing new technologies.

Godiva (Food). http://www.godiva.com/
"World of Chocolate," plus romances, horoscope, and online shopping.

Goodyear (Chemicals). http://www.goodyear.com/
Learn more about Goodyear's flagship product at this "tire school."

Home Depot (Hardware/Furnishings). http://www.homedepot.com
News, entironmental and community service information, and a direct purchase program from this home center retailer.

IBM (Computers). http://www.ibm.com
IBM news, products, and "other voices" on the effects of information technology.

ITT Hartford (Insurance). http://www.thehartford.com
Products and services, investment profiles, and news and issues.

JC Penney (Retail). http://www.jcpenney.com
Cybershop, get decorating tips, and enter contests at this retail site.

Kmart (Retail). http://www.kmart.com
Kmart's history, news, plus shopping.

Kodak (Photography). http://www.kodak.com
Info on photography, digital photography, and Kodak products.

Marriott (Hospitality). http://www.marriott.com
Traveler's companion, plus an overview of Marriott services.

Master Lock (Security). http://www.masterlock.com
Contests, security tips, plus fun security facts.

MCI (Telecommunications). http://www.mci.com
Provides global connections, a guide to 'Net resources, and more.

Mobil (Petroleum). http://www.mobil.com
Site includes special programs, including racing and literature prizes.

Motorola (Electronics). http://www.motorola.com/
Product portfolio, business news, and access to Motorola's "global community."

MTV (Entertainment). http://www.mtv.com
Live news flashes across your screen at this up-to-the-minute entertainment site.

Paramount Pictures (Entertainment). http://www.paramount.com/
Paramount's latest motion picture, TV, video, and digital entertainment releases.

Pizza Hut (Food). http://www.pizzahut.com
Order pizza online.

Price Costco (Retail). http://www.pricecostco.com
Visit small business, corporate, and product zones, or enter to win $100 for the stupidest customer question.

Sony (Entertainment and Electronics). http: www.sony.com
Games, shopping, and product information.

Sprint (Telecommunications). http://www.sprint.com
"Druper's House" features advice and services geared toward college students.

Texaco (Petroleum). http://www.texaco.com
Job opportunities, campus visit schedules, scholarship info, and more in the "on-campus" section.

Time Warner (Entertainment and Media). http://www.pathfinder.com
Access this entertainment conglomerate's various publications via the Internet.

Toys "R" Us (Toys). http://www.tru.com/
Find out about employment opportunities, explore a "funzone," or go on a "field trip Friday."

United Airlines (Transportation). http://www.ual.com
Company info, news, and travel tips.

United Parcel Service (Shipping). http://www.ups.com
Includes a "career mosaic" for employment opportunities.

High School Calendar

To help you and your high schooler start making the most of her four years, here's a year-by-year calendar. Depending on your child's personal style and needs, you may want to give the calendar to her to read, or simply help her plan for and tackle activities and events as they arise.

FRESHMAN YEAR

Now is the time to start gathering information about what your high school offers, as well as planning a schedule for the upcoming four years.

Fall

- Meet with your guidance counselor. Get copies of the courses offered, the requirements for graduation, and an explanation of the grading system.
- Draft a four-year schedule of classes that meet the minimum requirements for college admission.
- Find out about the extracurricular activities available at your school. Talk to student advisors and coaches about your options.
- Draft a four-year schedule of athletic and extracurricular activities you'd like to become involved in.
- Build a schedule that will accommodate time for studying, extracurricular activities, working out, and relaxing.

Spring

- Set a goal to get higher grades in all of the key subject areas (English, math, science, history, foreign language).
- Begin a vocabulary-building program.
- Look into work, study, or sports summer programs.

Summer

- Volunteer some time to a local group, such as a summer day camp or clean-up organization.
- Find informal or organized ways to purse your extracurricular and athletic interests.
- Read at least four books.
- Keep up a general level of physical fitness.

SOPHOMORE YEAR

This year, focus on building your academic skills. Continue to pursue the extracurricular activities that interest you most.

Fall

- Update your four-year class schedule. Make sure that you are meeting the minimum requirements for college admissions, and you are on track to complete most of the requirements be the end of your junior year.
- Update your four-year athletic and extracurricular calendar. Have you set, and are you meeting, specific goals?
- Register for the PSAT/NMSQT (you may have to contact your guidance counselor directly if your school only automatically registers juniors for the test).
- Take the PSAT (given only once in October)
- If you are pursuing a sport seriously, research its NCAA requirements. Plan an academic and athletic program that allows you to maintain eligibility for NCAA programs.

Spring

- Take the SAT IIs in the courses and key areas in which you have completed the last course for high school study, have done well (B+ average or better), and have an interest.
- Continue to set and achieve the goal of getting higher grade averages in the key subject areas.
- Identify work, study, and/or athletic programs that you can become involved in this summer.

Summer

- Continue to sharpen your basic math and vocabulary skills through a self-study or organized study program.
- Read at least four books.
- Involve yourself in at least one organized work, athletic, or study program this summer.

JUNIOR YEAR

During your junior year, you'll really need to gear up for the college application process. It's a crucial year in your high school career.

Fall

- Register for the PSAT/NMSQT.
- Take the PSAT/NMSQT in October. (This time it counts).
- Begin the college search process: Identify the criteria that are important to you; match these criteria to colleges (through books, software, or online search programs); generate a list of no more than 20 schools that appear to meet your criteria. Write to these schools and request an application with related information for admissions.
- If playing sports in college is a goal, write to college coaches for your sport at your target schools. Send them a note describing your interest in their school's program and your experience in the sport (including years played, training, stats, and special honors and awards). Also include a schedule of activity for the upcoming year (intercollegiate calendar, local and other tournaments, special camps and programs). Register with the NCAA Initial-Eligibility Clearinghouse.

- Attend local college fairs, and begin visiting your target schools if at all possible. Introduce yourself to the college advisor at your school if it will be someone other than your guidance counselor. Ask about the schedule of visiting recruiters, and circle the dates for recruiters visiting from your target schools.

- Summarize the academic requirements that apply to your schools. Compare them to your course schedule. Adjust your course schedule (if necessary) to be sure that you can meet the academic requirements of your target schools.

- Identify what the test requirements are for your target schools (e.g., SAT I scores, ACT scores, SAT II scores, and/or other). When you receive your PSAT scores, add a zero to each (so that a 58 becomes a 580). Match your PSAT scores to the SAT I score averages for your target schools. Are you at or above these averages? Continue to polish your math and verbal/reading skills, and you should continue to be in great shape.

- Begin preparing for the SAT I. If you're within 50 points of the average scores, at minimum, purchase a book and self-study for the SAT I. If you are more than 50 points away on the math and/or verbal scores, undertake a formal course of study, through books, software, or a course. Start your study program in January so you can build and practice the skills you need before the May test date.

- If many of your target schools require the ACT, begin preparing for it, and determine whether your remaining schools will accept the ACT instead of the SAT I.

- Request financial aid bulletins from all of your target schools. Estimate the college costs, and begin to identify the ways in which you and your family will meet them. Get a copy of the FAFSA and take your family through the process of completing one. Use one of the software and/or online programs to estimate your Expected Family Contribution.

- Begin searching for scholarship programs that you will be eligible for. Collect and prepare drafts of the application materials. Draft a schedule of deadline dates so you can be best prepared to meet them next year.

Spring

- Complete your study for the SAT I or ACT.
- Take the SAT I in March (if you are at or over your target SAT I score) or

May (if you need to prepare for the SAT I to improve your scores), or take the ACT.

- Take the SAT IIs in the courses and key areas in which you have completed the last course for high school study, have done well (B+ average or better), and have an interest.
- Take the AP for those AP or college-level courses you will complete this spring.
- Check with your guidance office to see if any representatives from your target schools are planning to visit your school. Sign up for these visits, and prepare any questions you may have to ask the visiting recruiter.
- Identify the organized study, work, or athletic program that you can become involved in this summer.

Summer

- Begin visiting colleges.
- Prepare drafts of your essays for your target schools.
- Become involved in at least one organized study, athletic, or work activity.
- Read at least four books.

SENIOR YEAR

Time to get serious about applying to college. It's especially important to keep yourself organized now, as you approach numerous application deadlines.

Fall

- Review your list of target schools. What are your chances of getting in? Make sure to include one safety school in your list.
- Review the admissions requirements one final time to make sure you meet the academic and testing requirements. Make adjustments to course schedule as needed.
- Take the SAT I or ACT again if you need higher test scores and have prepared over the summer to improve them.
- Meet with visiting recruiters from your target schools.
- If you'll be pursuing athletics at college, make telephone contact with the

coaches at your target schools. Update your athletic résumé, and keep coaches up-to-date on your latest activities and schedules. Find out the Letter of Intent dates for your sport from the NCAA.

- Send for the application materials. Also request information on financial aid. Note the application and financial aid deadlines.
- Send for the application materials for your targeted scholarship and grant programs. Make sure that you meet the eligibility requirements for each program.
- Visit the campuses on your list of targets.
- Identify at least two teachers and two extracurricular advisors (e.g., coach and employer) who could write solid, glowing recommendations for you. Approach them and discuss where you will be applying, why, and your desire to have them support your application through a great recommendation about your character, contributions, and ability.
- Complete your school and scholarship applications. Have someone who has great English skills (such as an English teacher) review your application and essays for correctness and neatness. Note that applications for admissions and scholarships are usually accepted beginning in November; for early decisions and priority consideration for scholarships, you must apply now.
- Get a copy of the Free Application of Federal Student Aid (FAFSA). The FAFSA is usually made available in November.
- Since many application deadlines for schools and scholarships fall in December, make sure your applications are in on time.

Spring

- Collect your family's financial documents. Sit down with your parents and complete the FAFSA. Submit the FAFSA soon after January 1 as possible. The FAFSA must be submitted by March 1 to qualify for most state aid. The deadline to qualify for fall federal aid is May 1.
- Check with your guidance counselor and the personnel at your target schools to be sure that you have all of the additional financial aid forms to complete to qualify for additional school, state, and private financial aid. Be sure to complete and submit these forms before the stated deadlines.

- Review your Student Aid Report (SAR) for accuracy and completeness. If there are any changes, make them now, and make a copy before submitting the form. Be sure that you have selected all of your target schools to receive a copy of the SAR.
- Decide the college or university that you will attend this fall. Check to be sure you have received both admissions and financial aid award letters. Notify your choice college of your decision to matriculate.
- Take SAT II exams if high scores will allow you to place out of academic requirements for entering freshman or will help you to place into advanced courses in subject areas you plan to pursue in college.
- Estimate your college costs and your sources of financial aid. If your sources of aid don't meet your estimated expenses for the upcoming year, begin investigating loan opportunities. Take time to estimate what your financial needs will be for the next four years (the gap between your financial resources and the estimated annual cost of college). Plan now for meeting this gap for each of the next four years.
- Take the AP for those AP or college-level courses you will complete this spring.
- Begin evaluating your housing options for the fall. If you plan to live off campus, May can be the best time to find an apartment near campus.

Summer

- Consider getting a summer job to earn money for your college expenses.
- Relax and congratulate yourself: You're on your way to the college of your choice.

U.S. College and University Internet Site Directory

Alabama

Alabama A&M U. http://www.aamu.edu
Alabama State U. http://www.alasu.edu
Athens State College. http://iquest.com/~athens
Auburn U. at Main Campus. http://www.auburn.edu
Auburn U. at Montgomery. http://www-biz.aum.edu
Birmingham-Southern College. http://www.bsc.edu
Columbia Southern U. http://www.colsouth.edu
Concordia College. http://www.cuis.edu/www/cus/cual.html
Faulkner U. http://www.faulkner.edu
Huntingdon College. http://www.huntingdon.edu
Jacksonville State U. http://jsucc.jsu.edu
Judson College. http://home.judson.edu
Samford U. http://www.samford.edu
Spring Hill College. http://shu.edu
Troy State U. http://asntsu.asn.net
Tuskegee U. http://www.tusk.edu
U. of Alabama at Birmingham. http://www.uab.edu
U. of Alabama at Huntsville. http://www.uah.edu
U. of Alabama at Tuscaloosa. http://www.ua.edu
U. of South Alabama. http://www.usouthal.edu
U. of North Alabama. http://www.una.edu
U. of West Alabama. http://www.westal.edu

Alaska

Alaska Pacific U. http://www.alaska.net/apu/
U. of Alaska at Main Campus. http://www.alaska.edu
U. of Alaska at Anchorage. http://orion.alaska.edu.cwis.html
U. of Alaska at Fairbanks. http://info.alaska.edu:70/25/ua/ua_fairbanks
U. of Alaska at Southeast. http://www.jun.alaska.edu

Arizona

Arizona State U. http://www.asu.edu
Arizona State U., East. http://www.asu.edu/east
Arizona State U., West. http://www.west.asu.edu
Arizona Western College. http://www.cc.az.us
Eastern Arizona College. http://www.eac.cc.uz.us
Embry-Riddle Aeronautical U. http://www.pr.erau.edu
Northern Arizona U. http://www.nau.edu
Tucson U. http://www.tucson.edu
U. of Arizona. http://www.arizona.edu
U. of Phoenix. http://www.uophx.edu
Western International U. http://www.wintu.edu

Arkansas

Arkansas State U. http://www.astate.edu
Harding U. http://www.harding.edu
Henderson State U. http://www.hsu.edu
Hendrix College. http://www.hendrix.edu
John Brown U. http://www.jbu.edu
Lyon College. http://www.lyon.edu
Ouachita Baptist U. http://www.obu.edu
Philander Smith College. http://www.philander.edu
Southern Arkansas U. gopher://192.231.213.22/
U. of Arkansas at Fayetteville. http://www.uark.edu
U. of Arkansas at Little Rock. http://www.ualr.edu
U. of Arkansas at Monticello. http://cotton.uamont.edu
U. of Central Arkansas. http://www.uca.edu
U. of the Ozarks. http://www.ozarks.edu

California

Antioch U. at Los Angeles. http://www.antiochla.edu
Azusa Pacific U. http://www.apu.edu
Bethany College. http://www.bethany.edu
Biola U. http://www.biola.edu
California Coast U. http://www.calcoastuniv.edu
California Institute of Technology. http://www.caltech.edu
California Institute of the Arts. http://www.calarts.edu
California Lutheran U. http://robles.callutheran.edu
California Maritime Academy. http://www.csum.edu
California National U. http://www.cnuas.edu
California Pacific U. http://www.groupweb.com/cpu/cpu.htm
California State U. at Chico. http://www.csuchico.edu
California State U. at Fresno. http://athena.lib.csufresno.edu/csuf.htm
California State U. at Fullerton. http://www.fullerton.edu
California State U. at Humboldt. http://www.humboldt.edu
California State U. at Long Beach. http://www.acs.csulb.edu
Californa State U. at Los Angeles. http://www.calstatela.edu
California State U. at Northridge. http://www.csun.edu
California State U. at Sacramento. http://www.csus.edu
California State U. at San Diego. http://www.sdsu.edu
California State U. at San Jose. http://www.sjsu.edu
California State U. at San Marcos. http://coyote.csusm.edu
California State U. at Sonoma. http://www.sonoma.edu
California State U. at Stanislaus. http://lead.csustan.edu
California Polytechnic State U. at Pomona. http://www.csupomona.edu
California Polytechnic State U. at San Luis Obispo. http://www.calpoly.edu
Chapman U. http://www.chapman.edu
Claremont McKenna College. http://www.mckenna.edu
College of Notre Dame. http://www.cnd.edu
Dominican College. http://www.dominican.edu
Golden Gate U. http://www.ggu.edu
Harvey Mudd College. http://www.hmc.edu
John F. Kennedy U. http://www.jfku.edu
La Sierra U. http://www.lasierra.edu
Loma Linda U. http://www.llu.edu
Loyola Marymount U. http://www.lmu.edu

Mills College. http://www.mills.edu
National U. http://www.nu.edu
New College of California. http://www.newcollege.edu
Occidental College. http://www.oxy.edu
Pacific Union College. http://www.puc.edu
Peace College. http://www.peace.edu
Pepperdine U. http://www.pepperdine.edu
Pitzer College. http://www.pitzer.edu
Platt College. http://www.platt.edu
Point Loma Nazarene College. http://192.147.249.89
Pomona College. http://www.pomona.edu
St. Mary's College of California. http://www.stmarys-ca.edu
San Francisco State U. http://www.sfsu.edu
Santa Clara U. http://www.scu.edu
Scripps College. http://www.scrippscol.edu
Sonoma State U. http://www.sonoma.edu
Sostern College. http://www.swc.cc.ca.us
Stanford U. http://www.stanford.edu
The Master's College and Seminary. http://www.masters.edu
U.S. International U. http://www.usiu.edu
U. of California at Berkeley. http://www.berkeley.edu
U. of California at Davis. http://www.ucdavis.edu
U. of California at Irvine. http://www.uci.edu
U. of California at Los Angeles. http://www.ucla.edu
U. of California at Riverside. http://www.ucr.edu
U. of California at San Diego. http://www.ucsd.edu
U. of California at San Francisco. http://www.ucsf.edu
U. of California at Santa Barbara. http://www.ucsb.edu
U. of California at Santa Cruz. http://www.ucsc.edu
U. of LaVerne. http://www.ulaverne.edu
U. of Redlands. http://www.uor.edu
U. of San Diego. http://www.acusd.edu
U. of San Francisco. http://www.usfca.edu
U. of Southern California. http://www.usc.edu
U. of the Pacific. http://www.uop.edu
Westmont College. http://www.westmont.edu
Whittier College. http://www.whittier.edu
Woodbury U. http://www.woodburyu.edu

Colorado

Colorado Christian U. http://www.ccu.edu
Colorado College. http://www.cc.colorado.edu
Colorado Mountain College. http://www.coloradomtn.edu
Colorado School of Mines. http://www.mines.edu
Colorado State U. http://www.colostate.edu
Fort Lewis College. http://www.fortlewis.edu
Mesa State College. http://www.mesa.colorado.edu
Metropolitan State College at Denver. http://www.mscd.edu
Regis U. http://www.regis.edu
U.S. Air Force Academy. http://www.usafa.af.mil
U. of Colorado at Boulder. http://www.colorado.edu
U. of Colorado at Colorado Springs. http://www.uccs.edu
U. of Colorado at Denver. http://cudenver.edu
U. of Denver. http://www.du.edu
U. of Northern Colorado. http://www.univnorthco.edu
Western State College. http://www.wsc.colorado.edu

Connecticut

Central Connecticut State U. http://neal.ctstateu.edu/wwwhome.html
Connecticut College. http://camel.cenncoll.edu
Eastern Connecticut State U. http://www.ecsu.ctstateu.edu
Fairfield U. http://www.fairfield.edu
Quinnipiac College. http://www.quinnipiac.edu
St. Joseph College. http://www.sjc.edu
Sacred Heart U. http://www.sacredheart.edu
Southern Connecticut State U. http://scwww.ctstateu.edu
Teikyo Post U. http://www.teikyopost.edu
Trinity College. http://www.trincoll.edu
U. of Bridgeport. http://www.bridgeport.edu
U. of Connecticut. http://www.uconn.edu
U. of Hartford. http://www.hartford.edu/uofhwelcome.html
U. of New Haven. http://www.newhaven.edu
Wesleyan U. http://www.wesleyan.edu
Western Connecticut State U. http://www.wcsu.ctstateu.edu
Yale U. http://www.yale.edu

Delaware

Delaware State U. http://www.dsu.edu
Goldey Beacom College. http://goldey.gbc.edu
U. of Delaware. http://www.udel.edu
Wesley College. http://www.wesley.edu
Wilmington College. http://www.wilmington.edu

District of Columbia

American U. http://www.american.edu
Catholic U. of America. http://www.cua.edu
Gallaudet U. http://www.gallaudet.edu
Georgetown U. http://www.georgetown.edu
George Washington U. http://www.gwis.circ.gwn.edu
Howard U. http://www.howard.edu
Marymount U. http://www.marymount.edu
Strayer College. http://www.strayer.edu
Trinity College. http://www.consortium.org/~trinity/home.htm

Florida

Barry U. http://www.barry.edu/barryhome.html
Eckerd College. http://www.eckerd.edu
Embry-Riddle Aeronautical U. http://www.db.erau.edu
Flagler College. http://www.flagler.edu
Florida A&M U. http://www.famu.edu
Florida Atlantic U. http://www.fau.edu
Florida Gulf Coast U. http://www.fgcu.edu
Florida Institute of Technology. http://www.fit.edu
Florida International U. http://nomadd.fiu.edu
Florida Memorial College. http://www.bridge.net/~irfmc/
Florida State U. http://www.fsu.edu
Jacksonville U. http://junix.ju.edu
Jones College. http://www.jones.edu
Miami Christian U. http://mcu.edu
New College. http://www.sar.usf.edu
Nova Southeastern U. http://alpha.acast.nova.edu
Palm Beach Atlantic College. http://www.pbac.edu
Pensacola Christian College. http://www.pcci.edu
Ringling School of Art and Design. http://www.rsad.edu

Rollins College. http://www.rollins.edu
Stetson U. http://www.stetson.edu
Troy State U. http://www.tsufl.edu
U. of Central Florida. http://www.ucf.edu
U. of Florida. http://www.ufl.edu
U. of Miami. http://www.ir.miami.edu
U. of North Florida. http://www.unf.edu
U. of Sarasota. http://www.sarasota-online.com/school/univ.html
U. of South Florida. http://www.usf.edu
U. of Tampa. http://www.utampa.edu
U. of West Florida. http://www.uwf.edu

Georgia

Agnes Scott College. http://scottlan.edu
Armstrong State College. http://www.armstrong.edu
Athens Area Technical Institute. http://www.athens1.athens.tec.ga.us
Augusta College. gopher://gopher.ac.edu/1
Brenan U. http://www.brenan.edu
Clark Atlanta U. http://www.cau.auc.edu
Clayton State College. http://www.csc.peachnet.edu
Emory U. http://www.cc.emory.edu/welcome.html
Gainesville College. gopher://gopher.gc.peachnet.edu/1
Georgia College. http://www.gac.peachnet.edu
Georgia Institute of Technology. http://www.gatech.edu
Georgia State U. http://www.gsu.edu
Georgia Southern U. http://www.gasou.edu
Georgia Southwestern College. http://gswrs6k1.gsw.peachnet.edu
Kennesaw State College. http://wwwcoles.kennesaw.edu
LaGrange College. http://www.lgc.peachnet.edu
Mercer U. http://www.mercer.peachnet.edu
Middle Georgia College. http://www.mgc.peachnet.edu
Morehouse College. http://144.125.128.1/
North Georgia College. http://www.ngc.peachnet.edu
Oglethorpe U. http://www.oglethorpe.edu
Paine College. http://www.paine.peachnet.edu
Southern College of Technology. http://www.sct.edu
Spelman College. http://www.auc.edu

Thomas College. http://www.thomas.edu
U. of Georgia. http://www.uga.edu
Valdosta State College. http://www.valdosta.peachnet.edu
Wesleyan College. http://www.wesleyan.peachnet.edu
West Georgia College. http://www.westga.edu

Hawaii

Brigham Young U. http://www.byuh.edu
Chaminade U. of Honolulu. http://www.pixi.com/~chaminad/
Hawaii Pacific U. http://www.hpu.edu
U. of Hawaii. http://www.hawaii.edu/uhinfo.html
U. of Hawaii at Hilo. http://www.uhh.hawaii.edu

Idaho

Albertson College. http://www.acofi.edu
Boise State U. http://www.idbsu.edu
Idaho State U. http://www.isu.edu
Lewis-Clark State College. http://www.lcsc.edu
Northwest Nazarene College. http://www.nnu.edu
U. of Idaho. http://uidaho.edu

Illinois

Augustana College. http://www.augustana.edu
Aurora U. http://www.aurora.edu
Blackburn College. http://www.mcs.net/~kwplace/bc
Bradley U. http://www.bradley.edu
College of St. Francis. http://www.stfrancis.edu
Columbia College of Chicago. http://www.colum.edu
Concordia U. http://www.cuis.edu/www/curf/home.html
DePaul U. http://www.depaul.edu
East-West U. http://www.eastwest.edu
Eastern Illinois U. http://www.eiu.edu
Elmhurst College. http://www.elmhurst.edu
Govenors State U. http://www.ecn.bgu.edu/users/gsunow/gsu
Greenville College. http://www.greenville.edu
Illinois Benedictine College. http://www.ibc.edu
Illinois College. http://hilltop.ic.edu/ic.html
Illinois Institute of Technology. http://www.iit.edu

Illinois State U. http://www.ilstu.edu
Illinois Weslesyan U. http://www.iwu.edu
Knox College. http://www.knox.edu
Lake Forest College. http://www.lfc.edu
Lewis U. http://www.lewisu.edu
Loyola U. of Chicago. http://www.luc.edu
Millikin U. http://www.millikin.edu
Monmouth College. http://pippin.monm.edu
National-Lewis U. http://nlu.nl.edu
North Central College. http://www.noctrl.edu
North Park College. http://www.npcts.edu
Northwestern U. http://www.acus.nwu.edu
Olivet Nazarene U. http://www.olivet.edu
Principia College. http://www.prin.edu
Quincy U. http://www.quincy.edu
Rockford College. http://www.rockford.edu
Rosary College. http://www.rosary.edu/
St. Xavier U. http://www.sxu.edu
School of the Art Institute of Chicago. http://www.artic.edu/saic/saichome.html
Southern Illinois U., Main Campus. http://www.siu.edu
Southern Illinois U. at Edwardsville. http://www.siue.edu
U. of Chicago. http://www.uchicago.edu
U. of Illinois at Chicago. http://www.uic.edu
U. of Illinois at Urbana-Champaign. http://www.cso.uiuc.edu
Western Illinois U. http://www.wiu.edu
Wheaton College. http://www.wheaton.edu

Indiana

Anderson U. http://www.anderson.edu
Ball State U. http://www.bsu.edu
Butler U. http://www.butler.edu
De Pauw U. http://www.depauw.edu
Earlham College. http://www.earlham.edu
Goshen College. http://www.goshen.edu
Grace College. http://www.grace.edu
Hanover College. http://www.hanover.edu/home.html
Huntington College. http://www.huntcol.edu

Indiana Institute of Technology. http://www.indtech.edu
Indiana State U. http://www.indstate.edu
Indiana U. Southeast. http://www.ius.indiana.edu
Indiana U. at Bloomington. http://www.indiana.edu/iub
Indiana U. at Kokomo. http://www.ink.indiana.edu
Indiana U., Purdue U. at Columbus. http://www.columbus.iupui.edu
Indiana U., Purdue U. at Ft. Wayne. http://www.ipfw.indiana.edu
Indiana U., Purdue U. at Indianapolis. http://www,iupoi.edu
Indiana U. at South Bend. http://smartnet.iusb.indiana.edu/homepage.html
Indiana U. Southeast at New Albany. http://www.ius.indiana.edu
Purdue U. http://www.purdue.edu
Purdue U. at Calumet. http://www.calumet.purdue.edu
Purdue U. at North Central. http://www.purduenc.edu
Purdue U. at West Lafayette. http://www.purdue.edu
Rose-Hulman Institute of Technology. http://www.rose-hulman.edu
St Joseph's College. http://www.saintjoe.edu
St. Mary's College. http://www.saintmarys.edu
Taylor U. http://www.tayloru.edu
Tri-State U. http://www.tristate.com
U. of Evansville. http://www.evansville.edu
U. of Indianapolis. http://www.uindy.edu
U. of Notre Dame. http://www.ud.edu
U. of Southern Indiana. http://www.usi.edu
Valpraraiso U. http://www.valpro.edu
Wabash College. http://www.wabash.edu

Iowa

Briar Cliff College. http://www.briar-cliff.edu
Buena Vista U. http://bvc.edu
Central College. http://www.central.edu
Clarke College. http://www.clarke.edu
Coe College. http://www.coe.edu
Cornell College. http://www.cornell-iowa.edu
Dordt College. http://www.dordt.edu
Drake U. http://www.drake.edu
Graceland College. http://www.graceland.edu
Grinnell College. http://www.grin.edu

Iowa State U. http://www.iastate.edu
Loras College. http://www.loras.edu
Luther College. http://www.luther.edu
Maharishi International U. http://www.miu.edu
Mount St. Clare College. http://www.clare.edu
Northwestern College. http://solomon.nwciowa.edu
St. Ambrose U. http://www.sau.edu/sau.html
Simpson College. http://www.simpson.edu
Teikyo Marycrest U. http://geraldine.mcrest.edu
U. of Dubuque. http://www.dbq.edu
U. of Iowa. http://www.uiowa.edu
U. of Northern Iowa. http://www.uni.edu/index.html
Upper Iowa U. http://www.uiu.edu
Wartburg College. http://www.wartburg.edu
William Penn College. http://www.upenn.edu

Kansas

Baker U. http://www.bakeru.edu
Benedictine College. http://www.benedictine.edu
Bethel College. http://www.bethelks.edu
Emporia State College. http://www.emporia.edu
Fort Hays State U. http://www.fhsu.edu
Friends U. http://www.friends.edu
Haskell Indian Nations U. http://www.haskell.edu
Kansas State U. http://www.ksu.edu
Kansas Wesleyan U. http://www.kwu.edu
Mid-America Nazarene College. http://www.manc.edu
Pittsburg State U. http://www.pittstate.edu
St. Mary College. http://www.smcks.edu
Southwestern College. http://www.www.sckans.edu
Tabor College. http://www.tabor.edu
U. of Kansas. http://kuttp.cc.ukans.edu/cwis/kufacts_start.html
Upper Iowa U. http://www.uiu.edu
Washburn U. http://www.wuacc.edu
Wichita State U. http://www.twsu.edu

Kentucky

Berea College. http://www.berea.edu
Campbellesville College. http://www.campbellsvil.edu
Center College. http://www.centre.edu
Cumberland College. http://cc.cumber.edu
Eastern Kentucky U. http://www.eku.edu
Georgetown College. http://www.gtc.georgetown.ky.us
Murray State U. http://www.mursuky.edu
Northern Kentucky U. http://www.nku.edu
Thomas More College. http://www.thomasmore.edu
Transylvania U. http://www.transy.edu
U. of Kentucky. http://www.uky.edu
U. of Louisville. http://www.louisville.edu
Western Kentucky U. http://www.wku.edu

Louisiana

American Coastline U. http://www.amercoastuniv.edu
Centenary College of Louisiana. http://alpha.centenary.edu
Dillard U. http://www.dillard.edu
Louisiana College. http://www.lacollege.edu
Louisiana State U. http://unix1.succ.lsu.edu
Louisiana State U. at Alexandria. http://www.lsua.edu
Louisiana State U. at Shreveport. http://www.lsus.edu
Louisiana Technical U. http://aurora.latech.edu
McNeese State U. http://www.mcneese.edu
Nicholls State U. http://server.nich.edu
Northeast Louisiana U. http://www.nlu.edu
Northewestern State U. of Louisiana. http://www.nsula.edu
Southeastern Louisiana U. http://www.selu.edu
Southern U. http://www.subr.edu
Summit U. of Louisiana. http://www.summitunivofla.edu
Tulane U. http://www.tulane.edu
U. of New Orleans. http://www.uno.edu
U. of Southwestern Louisiana. http://www.usl.edu
Xavier U. of Louisiana. http://www.xula.edu

Maine

Bates College. http://www.bates.edu
Bowdoin College. http://www.bowdoin.edu
Colby College. http://www.colby.edu
College of the Atlantic. http://www.coa.edu
Husson College. http://www.husson.edu
Maine Maritime Academy. http://www.state.me-us/maritime/mma-htm
St. Joseph's College. http://www.sjcme.edu
Thomas College. http://www.thomas.edu/www/admiss/
U. of Maine at Farmington. http:///www.umf.maine.edu
U. of Maine at Fort Kent. http://ww.umfk.maine.edu
U. of Maine at Machias. http://www.umm.maine.edu
U. of Maine at Orono. http://www.kremer.ume.maine.edu/umorono.htm
U. of Maine at Presque Isle. http://www.umpi.maine.edu
U. of New England. http://www.une.edu
U. of Southern Maine. http://www.usm.maine.edu

Maryland

Bowie State U. http://www.bsu.umd.edu
Chesapeake College. http://www.chesapeake.edu
Columbia Union College. http://www.cuc.edu
Coppin State College. http://wwcoeacl.coppin.umd.edu
Frostburg State U. http://www.fsu.umd.edu
Goucher College. http://www.goucher.edu
Hood College. http://www.hood.edu
Johns Hopkins U. http:///www.jhu.edu
Loyola College. http://www.loyola.edu
Maryland Institute of Art. http://www.mica.edu
Morgan State U. http://www.morgan.edu
Mount St. Mary's College. http://msmary.edu
St. John's College. http://www.sjca.edu/admissions
Salisbury State U. http://www.ssu.umd.edu
Towson State U. http://www.towson.edu
U.S. Naval Academy. http://www.nadn.navy.mil/
U. of Baltimore. http://www.ubalt.edu
U. of Maryland Baltimore County. http://www.umbc.edu
U. of Maryland at College Park. http://www.umcp.umd.edu

Villa Julie College. http://www.vjc.edu
Washington College. http://www.washcoll.edu
Western Maryland College. http://www.umc.car.md.us

Massachusetts

American International College. http://www.aic.edu
Amherst College. http://www.amherst.edu
Assumption College. http://www.assumption.edu
Atlantic Union College. http://ww.atlanticuc.edu
Babson College. http://www.babson.edu
Bentley College. http://www.bentley.edu
Berklee College of Music. www.berklee.edu
Boston College. http://infoeagle.bc.edu
Boston U. http://www.bu.edu
Brandies U. http://www.brandeis.edu
Clark U. http://www.clarku.edu
College of the Holy Cross. http://www.holycross.edu
Curry College. http://www.curry.edu
Eastern Nazarene College. http://www.enc.edu
Emerson College. http://www.emerson.edu
Emmanuel College. http://www.emmanuel.edu
Fitchburg State College. http://www.fsc.edu
Framingham State College. http://www.frc.mass.edu
Gordon College. http://www.gordonc.edu
Hampshire College. http://www.hampshire.edu
Harvard U. http://www.harvard.edu
Massachusetts Maritime Academy. http://www.mma.mass.edu
Massachusetts Institute of Technology. http://www.mit.edu/admissions/www
Mount Holyoke College. http://www.myholyoke.edu
North Adams State College. http://www.nasc.mass.edu
Northeastern U. http://www.neu.edu
Simmons College. http://www.simmons.edu
Simon's Rock College of Bard. http://www.simons-rock.edu
Smith College. http://www.smith.edu
Stonehill College. http://www.stonehille.edu
Suffolk U. http://www.suffolk.edu
Tufts U. http://www.tufts.edu

U. of Massachusetts at Amherst. http://www.umass.edu
U. of Massachusetts at Dartmouth. http://www.umassd.edu
U. of Massachusetts at Lowell. http://www.uml.edu
Wellesley College. http://www.wellesley.edu
Wenworth Institute of Technology. http://www.wit.edu
Western New England College. http://www.wnec.edu
Westfield State College. http://www.wsc.mass.edu
Wheaton College. http://www.wheatonma.edu
Williams College. http://www.williams.edu
Worcester Polytechnic Institute. http://www.wpi.edu

Michigan

Albion College. http://www.albion.edu
Alma College. http://www.cc.alma.edu
Andrews U. http://www.cs.andrews.edu
Aquinas College. http://www.aquinas.edu
Calvin College. http://www.calvin.edu
Central Michigan U. http://cmuvm.csv.cmich.edu
Concordia College at Ann Arbor. http://www.ccaa.edu
Cornerstone College. http://www.grfn.org/~cstone/
Delta College. http://www.delta.edu
Eastern Michigan U. http://www.emich.edu
Ferris State U. http://www.ferris.edu/homepage/htm
Grand Valley State U. http://www.gvsu.edu
Hillsdale College. http://www.hillsdale.edu
Hope College. http://www.hope.edu
Kalamazoo College. http://www.kzoo.edu
Lake Superior State U. http://www.lssu.edu
Lawrence Technological College. http://www.ltu.edu
Michigan State U. http://www.msu.edu
Michigan Technological U. http://www.mtu.edu
Northwestern Michigan U. http://www.nmu.edu
Oakland U. http://www.acs.oakland.edu
Saginaw Valley State U. http://tardis.svsu.edu
Siera Heights College. http://www.sierahts.edu
Spring Arbor College. http://www.arbor.edu
U. of Detroit Mercy. http://www.udmercy.edu

U. of Michigan at Ann Arbor. http://www.umich.edu
U. of Michigan at Dearborn. http://www.umd.umich.edu
Wayne State U. http://www.wayne.edu
Western Michigan U. http://www.wmich.edu

Minnesota

Augsburg College. http://www.augsburg.edu
Bemidji State U. http://bsuweb.bemidji.msus.edu
Carleton College. http://www.carelton.edu
College of St. Benedict. http://www.csbsju.edu
College of St. Catherine. http://www.stkate.edu
College of St. Scholastica. http://www.css.edu
Concordia College at Moorehead. http://http://www.cord.edu
Concordia College at St. Paul. http://www.csp.edu
Gustavus Adolphus College. http://www.gac.edu
Hamline U. http://www.hamline.edu
Macalaster College. http://www.macalstr.edu
Mankato State U. http://mankato.msus.edu
Minnesota College of Art and Design. http://www.mcad.edu
Metropolitan State U. http://www.metro.msus.edu
Moorhead State U. http://mhd2.moorhead.msus.edu/cwis/mcucwis.start.html
Northwestern College. http://nwc.edu
St. Cloud State U. http://www.stcloud.msus.edu
St. John's U. http://www.csbju.edu
St. Mary's College. http://www.mnsmc.edu
St. Mary's U. http://www.smumn.edu
St. Olaf College. http://www.stolaf.edu
Southwest State U. http://www.southwest.msus.edu
U. of Minnesota. http://www.umn.edu
U. of Minnesota at Crookston. http://www.crk.umn.edu
U. of Minnesota at Duluth. http://www.d.umn.edu
U. of Minnesota at Morris. http://www.mrs.umn.edu
U. of Minnesota at Twin Cities. http://www.umn.edu
U. of St. Thomas. http://www.stthomas.edu
Walden U. http://www.walden.edu
Winona State U. http://gopher.winona.msus.edu

Mississippi

Delta State U. http://dsu2.deltast.edu
Jackson State U. http://ccaix.jsums.edu
Milsaps College. http://www.millsaps.edu
Mississippi College. http://www.mc.edu
Mississippi State U. http://www.msstate.edu
Mississippi U. for Women. http://muw.edu
U. of Mississippi. http://www.olemiss.edu
U. of Southern Mississippi. http://www.usm.edu

Missouri

Avila U. http://www.avila.edu
Baptist Bible College. http://www.seebc.edu
Central Methodist College. http://cmc2.cmc.edu
Central Missouri State U. http://cmsuvmb.cmsu.edu
College of the Ozarks. http://www.cofo.edu
Concordia College at St. Paul. http://www.csp.edu
Culver-Stockton College. http://www.culver.edu
Drury College. http://www.drury.edu
Fontbonne College. http://www.fontbonne.edu
Greenleaf U. http://www.greenleaf.edu
Lincoln U. http://www.lincolnu.edu
Mineral Area College. http://www.mac.cc.mo.us
Missouri Southern State College. http://www.mssc.edu
Missouri Western State College. http://www.mwsc.edu
Northeast Missouri State U. http://www.nemostate.edu
Northwest Missouri State U. http://nwmissouri.edu
Rockhurst College. http://vax1.rockhurst.edu
St. Louis U. http://www.slu.edu
Southeast Missouri State U. http://www.semo.edu
Southwest Baptist U. http://bearcat.sbuniv.edu
Southwest Missouri State U. http://www.smsu.edu
Stephens College. http://www.stephens.edu
U. of Missouri at Columbia. http://www.missouri.edu
U. of Missour at Kansas City. http://www.umkc.edu
U. of Missouri at Rolla. http://www.umr.edu
U. of Missouri at St. Louis. http://www.umsl.edu

Washington U. http://www.wustl.edu
Westminster U. http://www.westminster-mo.edu
William Jewell College. http://www.jewell.edu
William Woods U. http://www.wmwoods.edu

Montana

Carroll College. http://www.carroll.edu
Montana State U. at Billings. http://www.msubillings.edu
Montana State U. at Bozeman. http://www.montana.edu
Montana State U. at Northern Havre. http://www.nmclites.edu
Mountain Tech U. http://www.mtech.edu
Rocky Mountain College. http://www.rocky.edu
Salish Kootenai College. http://www.skc.edu
U. of Montanna. http://www.umt.edu
Western Montana College. http://www.wmc.edu

Nebraska

Chadron State College. http://www.csu.edu
Concordia College at Seward. http://ccsn.edu
Creighton U. http://www.creighton.edu
Dana College. http://www.dana.edu
Doane College. gopher://doane.edu/
Hastings College. http://www.hastings.edu
Peru State College. http://www.peru.edu
U. of Nebraska at Kearney. http://www.unk.edu
U. of Nebraska at Lincoln. http://www.unl.edu
U. of Nebraska at Omaha. http://www.unomaha.edu

Nevada

U. of Nevada Las Vegas. http://www.unlv.edu
U. of Nevada at Reno. http://www.unr.edu

New Hampshire

Antioch New England. http://www.antiochne.edu
Daniel Webster College. http://www.dwc.edu/
Dartmouth College. http://www.dartmouth.edu
Franklin Pierce College. http://www.fpc.edu
Keene State College. http://www.keene.edu

New Hampshire College. http://www.nhc.edu
Plymouth State College. http://www.plymouth.edu
Rivier College. http://www.riv.edu
Saint Anslem College. http://www.anslem.edu
Thomas Moore College. http://www.thomasmoore.edu
U. of New Hamphire, Dunham. http://www.unh.edu

New Jersey

College of New Jersey. http://www.trenton.edu
Drew U. http://www.drew.edu
Fairleigh Dickinson U. http://www.fdu.edu
Georgian Court College. http://www.georgian.edu
Kean College. http://www.kean.edu
Monmouth U. http://www.monmouth.edu
Montclair State College. http://www.montclair.edu
New Jersey Institute of Technology. http://www.njit.edu
Princeton U. http://www.princeton.edu
Ramapo College. http://www.ramapo.edu
Richard Stockton College. http://loki.stockton.edu/index.html
Rider U. http://www.rider.edu
Rowan College. http://www.rowan.edu
Rutgers State U. at Camden. http://camden-www.rutgers.edu
Rutgers State U. at New Brunswick. http://www.rutgers.edu
Rutgers State U. at Newark. http://www.rutgers.edu/newark
Seton Hall U. http://www.shu.edu
Stevens Institute of Technology. http://www.stevens-tech.edu
Thomas Edison State College. http://www.tesc.edu
William Paterson College. http://pioneer.wilpaterson.edu

New Mexico

Eastern New Mexico U. http://www.enmu.edu
New Mexico Highlands U. http://www.nmhu.edu
New Mexico Institute of Mining and Technology. http://www.nmt.edu
New Mexico State U. http://www.nmsu.edu
St. John's College. http://www.sjcsf.edu
San Juan College. http://www.sjc.cc.nm.es
U. of New Mexico, Main Campus. http://www.unm.edu
Western New Mexico U. http://www.wnmu.edu

New York

Adelphi U. http://www.adelphi.edu
Alfred U. http://www.alfred.edu
Bank Street College. http://www.bnkst.edu
Bard College. http://www.bard.edu
Barnard College. http://ultimate.barnard.columbia.edu
Canisius College. http://www.canisius.edu
Christian Leadership U. http://www.cluniv.edu
City University of New York (CUNY), Baruch College.
http://www.baruch.cuny.edu
CUNY, Brooklyn College. http://www.brooklyn.cuny.edu
CUNY, City College of New York. http://www.ccny.cuny.edu
CUNY, College of Staten Island. http://www.csi.cuny.edu
CUNY, Hunter Colllege. http://www.hunter.cuny.edu
CUNY, John Jay College. http://www.jjay.cuny.edu
CUNY, Lehman College. http://www.lehman.cuny.edu
CUNY, Queens College. http://www.qc.edu
Clarkson U. http://www.clarkson.edu
Colgate College. http://www.colgate.edu
College of Saint Rose. http://www.strose.edu
Columbia U. http://www.columbia.edu
Cooper Union. http://www.cooper.edu
Cornell U. http://www.cornell.edu
Culinary Institute of America. http://www.ciachef.edu/cia.html
Daemen College. http://www.daemen.edu
Dowling College. http://www.dowling.edu
Fordham U. http://www.fordham.edu
Hamilton College. http://www.hamilton.edu
Hartwick College. http://www.hartwick.edu
Hobart and William Smith Colleges. http://hws3.hws.edu:9000
Hofstra U. http://www.hofstra.edu
Iona College. http://www.iona.edu
Ithaca College. http://www.ithaca.edu
Keuka College. http://www.keuka.edu
Le Moyne College. http://www.lemoyne.edu
Manhattan College. http://www.mancol.edu
Marist College. http://www.marist.edu

Marymount College at Tarrytown. http://www.marymt.edu
Molloy College. http://www.molloy.edu
Mount St. Mary College. http://www.msmc.edu
Nazareth College of Rochester. http://www.naz.edu
New School for Social Research. http://dialnsa.edu/home/.html
New York Institute of Technology. http://www.nyit.edu
New York U. http://www.nyu.edu
Niagara U. http://www.niagara.edu
Pace U. http://www.pace.edu
Polytechnic U. http://www.poly.edu
Pratt Institute. http://www.pratt.edu
Rensselaer Polytechnic Institute. http://www.rpi.edu
Rochester Institute of Technology. http://www.rit.edu
Rockefeller U. http://www.rockefeller.edu
Russell Sage College. http://www.sage.edu
St. Bonaventure U. http://www.sbu.edu
St. John Fisher College. http://www.sjfc.edu
St. John's U. http://oghom.stjohns.edu
St. Lawrence U. http://music.stlawu.edu
Sarah Lawrence College. http://www.slc.edu
Skidmore College. http://www.skidmore.edu
State Univeristy of New York (SUNY) at Albany. http://csc.mosaic.albany.edu
SUNY at Alfred. http://www.alfredteh.edu
SUNY at Binghamton. http://www.binghamton.edu
SUNY at Brockport. http://www.brockport.edu
SUNY at Buffalo. http://www.wings.buffalo.edu
SUNY at Cobleskill. http://www.cobleskill.edu
SUNY at Cortland. http://www.cortland.edu
SUNY, Empire State College. http://www.esc.edu
SUNY, Environmental Science and Forestry. http://www.esf.edu
SUNY at Farmingdale. http://www.farmindale.edu
SUNY at Fredonia. http://www.cs.fredonia.edu
SUNY at Geneseo. http://mosaic.cc.geneseo.edu
SUNY, Institute of Technology. http://www.sunyit.edu
SUNY at Morrisville College. http://www.snymor.edu
SUNY at New Paltz. http://www.newpaltz.edu
SUNY at Oneonta. http://www.oneonta.edu
SUNY at Oswego. http://www.oswego.edu

SUNY at Plattsburg. http://www.plattsburg.edu
SUNY at Potsdam. http://www.potsdam.edu
Syracuse U. http://cwis.syr.edu
U.S Merchant Marine Academy. http://www.usmma.edu
U.S Military Academy. http://www.eecs.usma.edu
Union College. http://www.union.edu
U. of Rochester. http://www.rochester.edu
Vassar College. http://www.vassar.edu
Wells College. http://www.wells.edu
Yeshiva U. http://yu1.yu.edu

North Carolina

Appalachian State U. http://www.acs.appstate.edu
Campbell U. http://www.campbell.edu
Davidson College. http://www.davidson.edu
Duke U. http://www.duke.edu
East Carolina U. http://ecuvax.cis.ecu.edu
Elizabeth City State U. http://www.ecsu.edu
Elon College. http://www.elon.edu
Fayetteville State U. http://www.fsufay.edu
Guilford College. http://www.guilford.edu
High Point U. http://acme.highpoint.edu
Jacksonville U. http://junix.ju.edu:72/
Johnson C. Smith U. http://www.jcsu.edu/index.html
Lenoir-Rhyne College. http://www.lrc.edu
Mars Hill College. http://www.mhc.edu
Meredith College. http://www.meredith.edu/meredith
Methodist College. http://www.apcnet.com/methodist/methodist.html
Montreat-Anderson College. http://montreat.edu
North Carolina Agricultural and Technical State U. http://www.ncat.edu
North Carolina State U. at Raleigh. http://www.ncsu.edu
North Carolina Wesleyan College. http://ncwc.edu
North Carolina Central U. http://thumper.acc.nccu.edu/
Pembroke State U. http://www.pembroke.edu
St. Andrews Presbyterian College. http://www.spac.edu
U. of North Carolina at Asheville. http://www.unca.edu
U. of North Carolina at Chapel Hill. http://unc.edu

U. of North Carolina at Charlotte. http://unccvm.uncc.edu
U. of North Carolina at Greensboro. http://www.uncg.edu
U. of North Calorina at Wilmington. http://www.uncwil.edu
Wake Forest U. http://www.wfu.edu
Warren Wilson College. http://www.warren-wilson.edu
Western Carolina U. http://ww.wcu.edu
Wingate U. http://www.wingate.edu

North Dakota

Dickinson State U. http://www.dsu.nodak.edu
Jamestown College. http://acc.jc.edu
Mayville State U. http://vcsu.nodak.edu/masu/home.html
Minolt State College. http://warp6.cs.misu.nodak.edu
North Dakota State U. at Bottineau. http://165.234.172.78/homepage.html
U. of North Dakota. http://www.und.nodak.edu
Valley City State U. http://www.vcsu.nodak.edu/vcsu/home.html

Ohio

Antioch College. http://college.antioch.edu
Ashland U. http://www.ashland.edu
Baldwin-Wallace College. http://www.baldwinw.edu
Bluffton College. http://www.bluffton.edu
Bowling Green State U. http://www.bgsu.edu
Case Western Reserve U. http://www.cwru.edu
Cedarville College. http://www.cedarville.edu
Cleveland Institute of Art. http://www.zdepth.com/cia
Cleveland State U. http://www.csuohio.edu
College of Wooster. http://www.wooster.edu
Denison U. http://www.denison.edu
Heidelberg College. http://www.heidelberg.edu
Hiram College. http://www.hiram.edu
John Carroll U. http://www.jcu.edu
Kent State U. http://www.kent.edu
Kenyon College. http:///www.kenyon.edu
Malone College. http://www.malone.edu
Marietta College. http://www.marietta.edu
Miami U. at Oxford. http://www.muohio.edu

Mount Union College. http://www.muc.edu/default.html
Mount Vernon Nazarene College. http://mission.munc.edu
Muskingum College. http://www.muskingum.edu/www/index.html
Oberlin College. http://www.oberlin.edu
Ohio Dominican College. http://www.odc.edu
Ohio Northern U. http://www.onu.edu
Ohio State U. http://www.acs.ohio-state.edu
Ohio State at Marion. http://beetle.marion.ohio-state.edu
Ohio U. http://www.ohiou.edu
Ohio Wesleyan U. http://www.owu.edu
Otterbein College. http://www.otterbein.edu
Union Institute. http://www.unioninstitute.edu
U. of Akron. http://news.uakron.edu
U. of Cincinnati. http://www.uc.edu
U. of Dayton. http://udayton.edu
U. of Toledo. http://www.utoledo.edu
Wilmington College. http://www.wilmington.edu
Wittenberg U. http://www.wittenberg.edu
Wright State U. http://www.wright.edu
Xavier U. gopher://xavier.xu.edu
Youngstown State U. http://www.ysu.edu

Oklahoma

Cameron U. http://www.cameron.edu
East Central U. http://student.ecok.edu
Langston U. http://www.lunet.edu
Northeast State U. http://www.nsuok.edu
Oklahoma Baptist U. http://www.okbu.edu
Oklahoma Christian U. http://www.oc.edu
Oklahoma City U. http://frodo.okcu.edu
Oklahoma State U. http://www.okstate.edu
Oral Roberts U. http://www.oru.edu
Phillips U. http://www.phillips.edu
Southern Nazarene U. http://www.snu.edu
U. of Central Oklahoma. http://www.ucok.edu
U. of Oklahoma. http://www.uoknor.edu
U. of Science and Arts of Oklahoma. http://mercur.usao.edu
U. of Tulsa. http://www.utulsa.edu

Oregon

Eastern Oregon State College. http://www.eosc.osshe.edu
George Fox College. http://www.gfc.edu
Lewis and Clark College. http://lclark.edu
Linfield College. http://www.linfield.edu
Oregon Institute of Technology. http://www.oit.osshe.edu
Oregon State U. http://www.orst.edu
Pacific U. http://www.pacificu.edu
Portland State. http://www.pdx.edu
Reed College. http://www.reed.edu
Southern Oregon State College. http://www.sosc.osshe.edu/
U. of Oregon. http://www.uoregon.edu
U. of Portland. http://www.up.edu
Warner Pacific College. http://www.warnerpacific.edu
Western Baptist College. http://www.wbc.edu
Western Oregon State College. http://osshe.edu
Willamette U. http://www.willamette.edu

Pennsylvania

Albright College. http://www.alb.edu
Allegheny College. http://www.alleg.edu
Allentown College. http://www.allencol.edu
Beaver College. http://www.beaver.edu
Bloomberg U. http://www.bloomu.edu
Bryn Mawr College. http://www.brynmawr.edu
Bucknell U. http://www.bucknell.edu
California U. http://www.cup.edu
Carnegie Mellon U. http://www.cmu.com
Chatham College. http:www.chatham.edu
Cheyney U. http://www.cheyney.edu
Clarion U. http://www.clarion.edu
Dickinson College. http://www.dickinson.edu
Drexel U. http://www.drexel.edu
Duquesne U. http://www.duq.edu
East Stroundsburg U. http://www.esu.edu
Edinboro U. http://www.edinboro.edu
Elizabethtown College. http://www.etown.edu

Franklin and Marshall College. http://www.fandm.edu
Gannon U. http://www.gannon.edu
Geneva College. http://www.geneva.edu
Gettysburg College. http://www.gettysburg.edu/gburg.html
Gwynedd Mercy College. http://www.gmc.edu
Hahnemann U. http://www.hahnemann.edu
Haverford College. http://www.haverford.edu
Indiana U. http://www.iup.edu
Juniata College. http://www.juniata.edu
Mansfield U. http://www.mnsfld.edu
Moravian College. http://www.moravian.edu
King's College. http://www.kings.edu
Kutztown U. http://www.kutztown.edu
Lafayette College. http://www.lafayette.edu
La Salle U. http://www.lasalle.edu
Lebanon Valley College. http://www.lvc.edu
Lehigh U. http://www.lehigh.edu
Lincoln U. http://www.lincoln.edu
Lock Haven U. http://lhup.edu
Lycoming College. http://lycoming.edu
Marywood College. http://ac.marywood.edu
Messiah College. http://meddiah.edu
Millersville U. http://marauder.millersv.edu
Penn State at Hazelton. http://www.hn.psu.edu
Penn State, Main Campus. http://www.psu.edu
Penn State at York. http://www.yk.psu.edu
Robert Morris College. http://www.robert-morris.edu
St. Joseph's U. http://www.sju.edu
Shippensburg U. http://www.ship.edu
Swarthmore College. http://raptor.sccs.swarthmore.edu/
Temple U. http://www.temple.edu
Thiel College. http:///shrsys.hsic.org
U. of Pennsylvania. http://www.upenn.edu
U. of Pittsburgh, Main Campus. http://www.pitt.edu
U. of Scranton. http://www.uofs.edu
Ursinus College. http://vader.ursinus.edu
Villanova U. http://www.ucis.vill.edu
Washington and Jefferson College. http://www.washjeff.edu

Waynesburg College. http://waynesburg.edu
West Chester U. http://www.wcupa.edu
Westminster College. http://www.westminster.edu
Widener U. http://shirley.cs.widener.edu
Wilkes U. http://www.wilkes.edu
York College. http://www.ycp.edu

Rhode Island

Brown U. http://www.brown.edu
Bryant College. http://www.bryant.edu
Johnson and Wales U. http://www.jwu.edu
Providence College. http://www.providence.edu
Rhode Island College. http://www.ric.edu
Rhode Island School of Design. http://www.risd.edu
Roger Williams U. http://www.rwu.edu
U. of Rhode Island. http://www.uri.edu

South Carolina

Allen U. http://www.icusc.org/allen/auhome.htm
Anderson College. http://www.icusc.org/anderson/achome.htm
Benedict College. http://www.icusc.org/benedict/bchome.edu
Bob Jones U. http://www.bju.edu
Charleston Southern U. http://www.icusc.org/chas_sou/cshome.htm
The Citadel. http://www.citadel.edu
Claflin College. http://www.icusc.org/claflin/cchome.htm
Clemson U. http://www.clemson.edu
Coker College. http://www.icusc.org/coker/cchome.htm
College of Charleston. gopher://ashley.cofc.edu/
Converse College. http://www.icusc.org/converse/cchome.htm
Erskine College. http://www.icusc.org/erskine/echome.htm
Furman U. http://www.furman.edu
Johnson and Wales U. http://www.jwu.edu
Limestone College. http://www.icusc.org/limestone/lchome.htm
Morris College. http://www.icusc.org/morris/mchome.htm
Newberry College. http://www.newberry.edu
North Greenfield College. http://www.icusc.org/n_greenv/nghome.htm
Presbyterian College. http://www.presby.edu

Southern Wesleyan U. http://www.icusc.org/s_wesley/swhome.htm
Spartanbrug Methodist College. http://www.icusc.org/spartanb/schome
U. of South Carolina. http://www.scarolina.edu
U. of South Carolina at Aiken. http://www.usca.scarolina.edu
U. of South Carolina at Columbia. http://www.csd.scarolina.edu
U. of South Carolina at Spartanburg. http://www.uscs.edu
U. of South Carolina at Sumter. http://www.uscsu.edu
U. of South Carolina at Union. http://web.csd.sc.edu
Voorhees College. http://www.icusc.org/voorhees/vahome.htm
Winthrop U. http://lurch.winthrop.edu/withrophomepage.html
Wofford College. http://www.wofford.edu

South Dakota

Augustana College. http://www.augie.edu
Black Hills State U. http://www.bhsu.edu
Dakota State U. http://www.dsu.edu
Dakota Wesleyan U. http://dwu.edu
Northern State U. http://www.northern.edu
South Dakota School of Mines and Technology. http://www.sdsmt.edu
South Dakota State U. http://www.sdstate.edu
U. of Sioux Falls. http://www.thecoo.edu
U. of South Dakota. http:///www.usd.edu

Tennessee

Austin Peay State U. http://www.apsu.edu
Belmont U. http://www.belmont.edu
Carson-Newman College. http://www.cn.edu
Christian Brothers U. http://www.cbu.edu
East Tennessee State U. http://etsu.east-tenn-st.edu/etsu.html
Fisk U. http://www.fisk.edu
King College. http://www.king-bristol.tn.us
Lee College. http://www.lee.edu
Middle Tennessee State U. http://www.mtsu.edu
Rhodes College. http://www.rhodes.edu
Southern College. http://www.southern.edu
State Technological Institute. gopher://stim.tech.tn.us:70/1
Tennessee Technological U. http://www.ttu.edu

Union U. http://www.uu.edu
U. of Memphis. http://www.memphis.edu
U. of Tennessee at Chattanooga. http://www.utc.edu
U. of Tennessee at Knoxville. http://www.utk.edu
U. of Tennessee at Memphis. http://www.utemem.edu
U. of Tennessee at Martin. http://www.utm.edu
U. of the South. http://www.sewanee.edu
Vanderbilt U. http://www.vanderbilt.edu

Texas

Abilene Christian U. http://www.acu.edu
Ambassador U. http://www.ambassador.edu
Angelo State U. http://www.angelo.edu
Austin College. http://www.austinc.edu
Baylor U. http://www.baylor.edu
Concordia College at Austin. http://www.cuis.edu/www/cus/cutx.html
Dallas Baptist U. http://www.dbu.edu
East Texas State U. http://www.etsu.edu
Hill College. http://hillcollege.hill-college.cc.tx.us
Incarnate Word College. http://www.iwctx.edu
Lamar U. http://www.lamar.edu
Lee College. http://www.lee.edu
LeTourneau U. http://www.letu.edu
Mc Murray U. http://mcm.acu.edu
Midwestern State U. http://www.mwsu.edu
Our Lady of the Lake U. http://www.ollusa.edu
Rice U. http://riceinfo.rice.edu
St. Edward's U. http://www.stedwards.edu
Sam Houston State U. http://www.shsu.edu
Schreiner College. http://www.hilconet.com/~schreiner/
Southern Methodist U. http://www.smu.edu
Southwest Texas State U. http://www.swt.edu
Southwestern Adventist College. http://www.swac.edu
Southwestern Assemblies of God U. http://www.sagu.edu
Southwestern U. http://www.southwestern.edu
Stephen F. Austin State U. http://www.sfasu.edu
Tarleton State U. http://www.tarleton.edu

Texas A&M at Bonfire. http://www.tamu.edu/bonfire
Texas A&M U. at College Station. http://www.tamu.edu
Texas A&M U. at Corpus Christi. http://www.tamucc.edu
Texas A&M U., International U. http://www.tamiu.edu
Texas A&M U. at Kingsville. http://www.tamuk.edu
Texas Christian U. http://www.tcu.edu
Texas State Technical College at Waco. http://www.tstc.edu
Texas Southern U. http://www.tsu.edu
Texas Tech U. http://www.ttu.edu
Texas Woman's U. http://www.twu.edu
Tomball College. http://www.nhmccd.cc.tx.us
Trinity U. http://www.trinity.edu
U. of Central Texas. http://www.vvm.com/uct
U. of Dallas. http://acad.udallas.edu
U. of Houston, Main Campus. http://www.uh.edu
U. of North Texas. http://www.unt.edu
U. of St. Thomas. http://basil.stthom.edu
U. of Texas at Arlington. http://www.uta.edu
U. of Texas at Austin. http://www.utexas.edu/office/admissions
U. of Texas at Brownsville. http://www.utb.edu
U. of Texas at Dallas. http://www.utdallas.edu
U. of Texas at El Paso. http://www.utep.edu
U. of Texas at Houston. http://www.uth.tmc.edu
U. of Texas, Pan American. http://www.panam.edu
U. of Texas at San Antonio. http://www.utsa.edu
U. of Texas at Tyler. http://www.uttyl.edu
West Texas A&M. http://www.wtamu.edu

Utah

Brigham Young U. at Provo. http://www.byu.edu
College of Eastern Utah. http://www.ceu.edu
Southern Utah U. http://www.suu.edu
U. of Utah. http://www.utah.edu/html_docs/uofu_home.html
Utah State U. http://www.usu.edu
Utah Valley State College. http://www.uvsc.edu
Weber State U. http://www.weber.edu
Westminster College. http://www.wcslc.edu

Vermont

Bennington College. http://www.bennington.edu
Castleton State College. http://www.csc.vsc.edu
Champlain College. http://www.champlain.edu
Goddard College. http://sun.goddard.edu
Lyndon State College. http://www.lsc.vsc.edu
Marlboro College. http://www.marlboro.edu
Middlebury College. http://www.middlebury.edu
Norwich U. http://www.norwich.edu
St. Michael's College. http://waldo.smcvt.edu
U. of Vermont. http://www.uvm.edu
Vermont Technical College. http://www.vtc.vsc.edu

Virginia

Averett College. http://www.averett.edu
Bridgewater College. http://www.bridgewater.edu
Christopher Newport U. http:///www.cnu.edu
Clinch Valley College. http://www.clinch.edu
College of William and Mary. http://www.wm.edu
Eastern Mennonite U. http://www.emu.edu
Emory and Henry College. http://www.emory-henry.emory.va.us
George Mason U. http://www.gmu.edu
Hampton U. http://www.cs.hampton.edu
Hollins College. http://www.hollins.edu
James Madison U. http://www.jmu.edu
Liberty U. http://www.liberty.edu
Longwood College. http://www.lwc.edu
Lynchburg College. http://www.lynchburg.edu
Marine Corps U. http://www-mcu.mqg.usmc.mil
Mary Baldwin College. http://www.mbc.edu
Marymount U. http://www.marymount.edu
Mary Washington College. http:///www.mwc.edu
Norfolk State U. http://cyclops.nsu.edu
Old Dominion U. http://www.odu.edu
Radford U. http://www.runet.edu
Randolph-Macon College. http://www.rmc.edu
Randolph-Macon Woman's College. http://www.rmwc.edu

Regent U. http://www.regent.edu
Roanoke College. http://www.roanoke.edu
Shenandoah U. http://www.su.edu
Sweet Briar College. http://www.sbc.edu
U. of Richmond. http://www.urich.edu
U. of Virginia. http:///www.virginia.edu
Virginia Commonwealth U. http://www.vcu.edu
Virginia Intermont College. http://www.vic.edu
Virginia Military Institute. http://www.vmi.edu
Virginia Polytechnic Institute. http://www.vt.edu
Virginia State U. http://www.vsu.edu
Virginia Tech. http://www.vt.edu
Virginia Theological U. http://www.globalad.com/vt/vtu.htm
Virginia Wesleyan College. http://www.vwc.edu
Washington and Lee U. http://www.wlu.edu

Washington

Antioch U. at Seattle. http://www.seattleantioch.edu
Bastyr U. http://www.bastyr.edu
Central Washington U. http://www.cwu.edu
City U. http://www.cityu.edu/inroads/welcome.html
Clark College. http://clark.edu
Eastern Washington U. http://www.ewu.edu
Evergreen State U. http://www.evergreen.edu
Gonzaga U. http://www.gonzaga.edu
Pacific Lutheran U. http://www.plu.edu
St. Martin's College. http://www.stmartin.edu
Seattle Pacific U. http://www.spu.edu
Seattle U. http://www.seattleu.edu
U. of Puget Sound. http://www/ups/edu
U. of Washington. http://www.washington. edu
Walla Walla College. http://www.wwc.edu
Washington State U. http://www.wsu.edu
Washington State U. at Vancouver. http://vancouver.wsu.edu
Western Washington U. http://www.wwu.edu
Whitman College. http://www.whitman.edu
Whitworth College. http://www.whitworth.edu

West Virginia

Alderson-Broaddus College. http://www.mountain.net/ab
Bethany College. http://info.bethany.wvnet.edu
Concord College. http://www.concord.wvnet.edu
Davis & Elkins College. http://www.dne.wvnet.edu/
Fairmont State College. http://www.fairmont.wvnet.edu
Marshall U. http://www.marshall.edu
Salem-Teikyo College. http://stulib.salem-teikyo.wvnet.edu
Shepherd College. http://www.shepherd.wvnet.edu
U. of Charleston. http://www.uchaswv.edu
West Liberty State College. http://www.wlsc.wvnet.edu
West Virginia Institute of Technology. http://www.wvitioe.wvnet.edu
West Virginia State College. http://www.wvsc.wvnet.edu/
West Virginia U. http://www.wvu.edu
West Virginia Wesleyan College. http://www.wvwc.edu
Wheeling Jesuit College. http://www.wsj.edu

Wisconsin

Alverno College. http://www.alverno.edu
Beloit College. http://stu.beloit.edu
Cardinal Stritch College. http://www.stritch.edu
Carroll College. http://www.carroll.com
Carthage College. http://www.carthage.com
Chippewa Valley Technical College. http://www.chippewa.tec.wi.us
Concordia U. http://www.cuw.edu
Edgewood College. http://www.edgewood.edu
Lawrence U. http://www.lawrence.edu
Madison Area Technical College. http://www.madison.tec.wi.us
Marquette U. http://www.mu.edu
Milwaukee Area Technical College. http://www.milwaukee.tec.wi.us
Milwaukee School of Engineering. http://www.msce.edu
Mount Senario College. http://www.mscfs.edu
Northland College. http://bobb.northland.edu
Ripon College. http://www.ripon.edu
St. Norbert College. http://138.74.138.16/home.html
U. of Wisconsin at Eau Claire. http://www.uwec.edu
U. of Wisconsin, Fox Valley Center. http://www.fox.uwc.edu

U. of Wisconsin at Green Bay. http://www.uwgb.edu
U. of Wisconsin at La Crosse. http://www.uwlax.edu
U. of Wisconsin at Madison. http://www.wisc.edu
U. of Wisconsin, Marathon Center. http://mthwww.uwc.edu
U. of Wisconsin at Milwaukee. http://www.uwm.edu
U. of Wisconsin at Oshkosh. http://www.uwosh.edu
U. of Wisconsin at Parkside. http://www.uwp.edu
U. of Wisconsin at Platteville. http://www.uwplatt.edu
U. of Wisconsin at River Falls. http://www.uwrf.edu
U. of Wisconsin at Stevens Point. http://www.uwsp.edu
U. of Wisconsin at Stout. http://www.uwstout.edu
U. of Wisconsin at Superior. http://www.uwsuper.edu
U. of Wisconsin at Whitewater. http://www.uww.edu

Wyoming

U. of Wyoming. http://www.uwyo.edu

How Did We Do? Grade Us.

Thank you for choosing a Kaplan book. Your comments and suggestions are very useful to us. Please answer the following questions to assist us in our continued development of high-quality resources to meet your needs.

The Kaplan book I read was: _____

My name is: _____

My address is: _____

_____

My e-mail address is: _____

What overall grade would you give this book? (A) (B) (C) (D) (F)

How relevant was the information to your goals? (A) (B) (C) (D) (F)

How comprehensive was the information in this book? (A) (B) (C) (D) (F)

How accurate was the information in this book? (A) (B) (C) (D) (F)

How easy was the book to use? (A) (B) (C) (D) (F)

How appealing was the book's design? (A) (B) (C) (D) (F)

What were the book's strong points? _____

How could this book be improved? _____

Is there anything that we left out that you wanted to know more about?

Would you recommend this book to others? ☐ YES ☐ NO

Other comments: _____

_____

_____

Do we have permission to quote you? ☐ YES ☐ NO

Thank you for your help. Please tear out this page and mail it to:

Dave Chipps, Managing Editor
Kaplan Educational Centers
888 Seventh Avenue
New York, NY 10106

Or, you can answer these questions online at www.kaplan.com/talkback.

Thanks!

SIXTY · YEARS · OF
KAPLAN
60
BUILDING · FUTURES

The 7 HABITS
of Highly Effective
TEENS

"Have you ever packed a suitcase and noticed how much more you can fit inside when you neatly fold and organize your clothes instead of just throwing them in? It's really quite amazing. The same goes for your life. If you are better organized, you'll be able to pack more in—more time for family and friends, more time for school, more time for yourself, more time for the things that matter most to you."

—Sean Covey

Franklin Covey, the global provider of leadership development and productivity services, has created products and programs to help you learn to balance school, work, and family life.

- ***The 7 Habits of Highly Effective Teens*** is the ultimate teenage success guide. Sean Covey applies the timeless principles of the 7 Habits to you and the tough issues and decisions you face every day. It provides hope for teens in any situation and in all walks of life.

- **The 7 Habits workshops for teens**—available soon through Kaplan Educational Centers

- The **Collegiate Planner**™ is the perfect tool for achieving what matters most in the most efficient way possible. Students that use planners tend to have higher GPA's and are more likely to graduate.

- The **What Matters Most**™ **workshop** goes far beyond traditional time management remedies like working harder and faster. At a What Matter Most workshop, you'll not only learn how to manage your time better, you'll also discover how to become more productive and accomplish the things that matter most to you.

For more information about these and other products and services provided by Franklin Covey, please call 1-800-952-6839 or visit our website at www.franklincovey.com.

Congratulations!

You've chosen the best guide to college admissions.

Now subscribe to Kaplan's free e-mail newsletter.

Every week you'll get valuable information delivered right to your e-mail box:

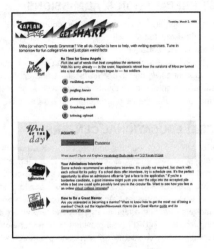

SAT, ACT, & PSAT Strategies

Powerful test-taking techniques

Reminders about upcoming tests and deadlines

Interactive vocabulary flashcards

Stress-busting exercises

College Admissions Advice

Expert admissions tips

Virtual road trips to colleges and universities

School selection information

Plus, every day you'll receive fun math, writing, or logic brainteasers that will help you improve your critical thinking skills.

Sign up today — it's free!

The Kaplan Edge
www.kaplan.com/edge

About KAPLAN
Educational Centers

Kaplan Educational Centers is one of the nation's leading providers of premier education and career services. Kaplan is a wholly owned subsidiary of The Washington Post Company.

TEST PREPARATION & ADMISSIONS

Kaplan's nationally recognized test prep courses cover more than 20 standardized tests, including secondary school, college and graduate school entrance exams and foreign language and professional licensing exams. In addition, Kaplan offers private tutoring and comprehensive, one-to-one admissions and application advice for students applying to graduate programs. Kaplan also provides information and guidance on the financial aid process.

SCORE! EDUCATIONAL CENTERS

SCORE! after-school learning centers help K-8 students build confidence, academic and goal-setting skills in a motivating, sports-oriented environment. Its cutting-edge, interactive curriculum continually assesses and adapts to each child's academic needs and learning style. Enthusiastic Academic Coaches serve as positive role models, creating a high-energy atmosphere where learning is exciting and fun. SCORE! Prep provides in-home, one-on-one tutoring for high school academic subjects and standardized tests.

KAPLAN LEARNING SERVICES

Kaplan Learning Services provides customized assessment, education and professional development programs to K-12 schools and universities.

KAPLAN INTERNATIONAL PROGRAMS

Kaplan services international students and professionals in the U.S. through a series of intensive English language and test preparation programs. These programs are offered at Kaplan City Centers and four new campus-based centers in California, Washington and New York via Kaplan/LCP International Institute. Kaplan and Kaplan/LCP offer specialized services to sponsors including placement at top American universities, fellowship management, academic monitoring and reporting, and financial administration.

KAPLAN PUBLISHING

Kaplan Publishing produces books, software and online services. Kaplan Books, a joint imprint with Simon & Schuster, publishes titles in test preparation, admissions, education, career development and life skills; Kaplan and Newsweek jointly publish guides on getting into college, finding the right career, and helping your child succeed in school. Through an alliance with Knowledge Adventure, Kaplan publishes educational software for the K-12 retail and school markets.

KAPLAN PROFESSIONAL

Kaplan Professional provides recruitment and training services for corporate clients and individuals seeking to advance their careers. Member units include Kaplan Professional Career Services, the largest career fair provider in North America; Perfect Access/CRN, which delivers software education and consultation for law firms and businesses; HireSystems, which provides web-based hiring solutions; and Kaplan Professional Call Center Services, a total provider of services for the call center industry.

DISTANCE LEARNING DIVISION

Kaplan's distance learning programs include Concord School of Law, the nation's first online law school; and National Institute of Paralegal Arts and Sciences, a leading provider of degrees and certificates in paralegal studies and legal nurse consulting.

COMMUNITY OUTREACH

Kaplan provides educational resources to thousands of financially disadvantaged students annually, working closely with educational institutions, not-for-profit groups, government agencies and other grass roots organizations on a variety of national and local support programs. Kaplan enriches local communities by employing high school, college and graduate students, creating valuable work experiences for vast numbers of young people each year.

Want more information about our services, products or the nearest Kaplan center?

Call our nationwide toll-free numbers:

1-800-KAP-TEST for information on our courses,
private tutoring and admissions consulting
1-800-KAP-ITEM for information on our books and software
1-888-KAP-LOAN* for information on student loans

Connect with us in cyberspace:

On AOL, keyword: kaplan
On the World Wide Web, go to: www.kaplan.com
Via e-mail: info@kaplan.com

Write to:

Kaplan Educational Centers
888 Seventh Avenue
New York, NY 10106